Walking to America

Walking to America

A Boyhood Dream

ROGER HUTCHINSON

BIRLINN

First published in 2009 by
Birlinn Limited
West Newington House
10 Newington Road
Edinburgh
EH9 1QS

www.birlinn.co.uk

ISBN: 978 1 84158 783 7

British Library Cataloguing-in-Publication Data
A catalogue record for this book is available from the British Library

Typeset by Iolaire Typesetting, Newtonmore
Printed and bound by CPI, Mackays, Chatham ME5 8TD

To Rosina, Ina and Rosie

Contents

THE KNOWN

Interlude

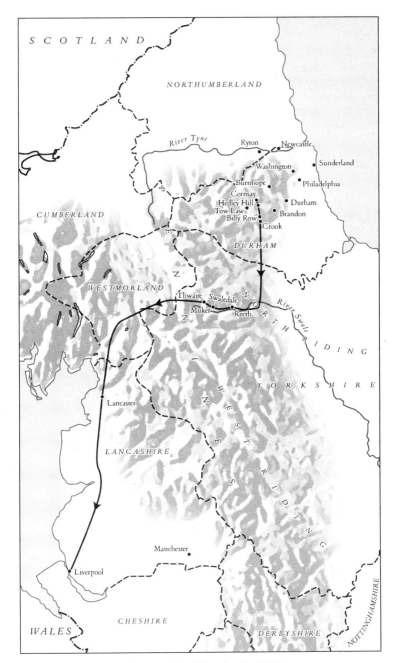

The North of England, 1883

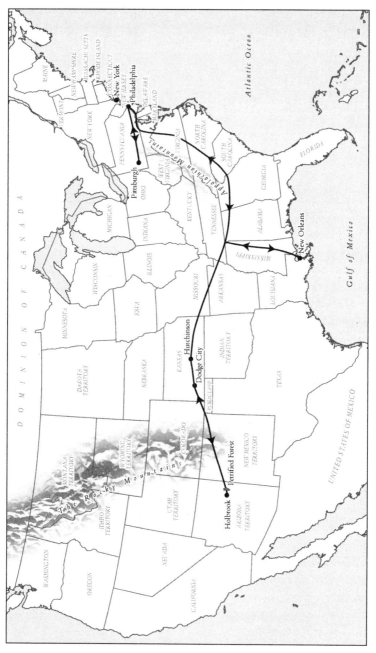

United States of America and territories, 1885

My father's father, whose name was William Hutchinson, was 31 years old when his only son was born. That son, my father, whose name was also William Hutchinson, was 35 when his new bride gave birth to me. This is not a riddle – add them up. They amount to the fact that I knew my grandfather, although he died at the good old age of 77, only in the last few years of his life and the first few sentient years of my own.

William Hutchinson was, in the second half of the 1950s, a retired collier. He lived in a small bungalow on the south bank of the River Tyne in north-eastern England. A Victorian by birth and upbringing, he adhered in the middle of the twentieth century to what I now recognise as the minor habits of the nineteenth-century working classes. He broke away the shells of soft-boiled eggs, tipped the white-and-yellow ooze into a bowl and sipped it from a spoon. He poured his morning tea firstly into a cup. He stirred sugar and milk into the cup and then transferred its contents to a deep saucer, held the saucer in both hands and drank the dark brown liquid carefully from the rim.

Those are the wide-eyed memories of the boy that I was when he died. I have few others. But among them is the impression that he seemed entirely housebound. He could walk, but rarely did. Some of his children had motorcars, but he never allowed himself to be taken out for a drive. There was a small front garden by his cottage, and beyond it a threadbare village green, but he never set foot in them. It seemed as though he had transferred, overnight, his working life underground to his retirement indoors, preferring even in the brief freedom of his eighth decade to stay away from the direct light of the day and the hubbub of the busy world on the surface of the earth.

If, unlike everybody else that this child knew, my grandfather never left his house, he did have one intriguing and entirely compensatory asset.

Unusually for a man of that class at that time, and doubly unusually for a man who in most other respects seemed to belong to a previous era (he did not own and might have had difficulty operating a telephone), he had a television. As we at home did not, that screen in my grandfather's cottage was the doorway to wonderland. I am not sure what he – sitting stiffly in his armchair – preferred to watch. Of course, as there were only two channels, the exercise of preference was, in the late 1950s and early 1960s, limited almost to having the TV set turned on or off. But I was entranced by every moving black-and-white image, from the puppet shows to the news bulletins and the glorious Hollywood movies.

So, like my grandfather, I spent my time at his cottage indoors, on the floor beside his armchair, absorbed in the television set as he sat enigmatically silent and still above me.

It was on one such occasion that another of the few episodes which drilled themselves into my memory occurred. An American made-for-television western was showing. I cannot remember which one it was. Wagon Train, perhaps, or Gunsmoke. There arrived a lull in the action, during which the camera panned lovingly down a wooded valley towards a plume of smoke wafting vertically through the still air. The source of that plume of smoke was a small log cabin, set alone in a glade, surrounded by rough timber fencing, studio-recreated in the frontier style.

My grandfather sat forward in his chair. He pointed an index finger at the screen and spoke to me his first words of the evening. (Of the day? Of the week? Of the month?)

'I used to live there,' he said.

THE KNOWN

1

Rest-Stops on the Road

Philadelphia, Pennsylvania, 1885

'For Disappointments, that come not by our own Folly, they are the Tryals or Corrections of Heaven: and it is our own Fault, if they prove not our Advantage.'

– *William Penn (1644–1718), founder of the Province of Pennsylvania and the city of Philadelphia.*

On a winter morning early in 1885 a young woman looked from the deck of the passenger steamer *British Crown* upon a new city whose name had haunted her since childhood. Rosina Hutchinson, her husband Miles, her brother-in-law Christopher, her baby son William – whose second birthday had occurred during the voyage from England – and their 139 shipmates were in pursuit of the fantasy of Philadelphia and the fertile interior of the state of Pennsylvania in the United States of America.

Rosina, William, Miles and Christopher Hutchinson were far from being alone. Twenty-seven thousand Europeans had already arrived in Philadelphia in the single year of 1884: about 500 men, women and children made unsteady landfall on the Delaware wharves each week. More than a quarter of the city's 800,000 population had been born outside the USA. Half of those 200,000 immigrants were Irish, 50,000 of them were German, and of the rest, perhaps 30,000 or 40,000, had travelled from England and Scotland.

Among them were three of Rosina's sisters, who had preceded her to Pennsylvania a year earlier. Two of them, Sarah and Rachel, had followed their husbands overland to Pittsburgh and the trumpeted employment opportunities of the western Pennsylvania coalfield.

The other sister, Kate, remained on the coast. Kate was blind, and she and her husband, Tom Wilkinson, were still in Philadelphia partly because Tom – a man who had registered his occupation as 'farmer' on the emigrant ship – had no immediate desire to resume his British occupation of coalmining, and partly because rich, sophisticated Philadelphia offered remedies for Kate's sightlessness which were unavailable in proletarian Pittsburgh.

Remarkably, the city and the state could accommodate the horde of immigrants, and most of their reveries. The continent of infinite opportunity was only just beginning properly to exploit itself.

Miles, Rosina, Christopher and William Hutchinson disembarked that winter's day at the very beginning of 1885 on a wharf at the foot of Philadelphia's Washington Avenue, to be met by Kate and Tom. The river behind them swarmed with three-masted schooners, two-funnelled steamers, yachts, ferries, and various sea and river-going mongrel hybrids of steam and sail. A small, wooded island with a handful of houses, the tall, smoking chimneys of manufactories and a couple of crumbling windmills stood a few hundred yards offshore. Half a mile beyond Windmill Island, at the opposite, eastern side of the Delaware River, there appeared to be a sparse rural settlement.

The Washington Avenue wharves were surrounded by 'warehouses, factories, sugar refineries, freight depots and grain elevators, all connected to the vast yards of the Pennsylvania Railroad'. The Hutchinson family entered the upper floor of a two-storey building and passed through a cursory customs inspection which was chiefly designed to confirm that they were neither paupers nor felons.

They then walked downstairs and out into a new world. Before them, as far as the eye could see, the orderly grid of Philadelphia's terraced streets stretched westward like a chequerboard. Horizontally, its pattern was broken hardly at all. Vertically, it was interrupted by a handful of mammoth civic and commercial towers. New buildings were rising on every corner; the roads rattled with horse-drawn streetcars and carriages and echoed with the abrupt shouts of working men.

Philadelphia coped in a couple of ways with the arrival of 20,000 to 30,000 foreigners on its doorstep every calendar year. Downstairs from the customs office in that two-storey building at Washington Avenue wharves was a railway ticket booth. Those many immigrants who had prearranged jobs elsewhere – as farmworkers, perhaps, or industrial labourers – could walk from the building straight into the Pennsylvania Railroad yard, onto a train and out of Philadelphia.

And as for the others, such as the Hutchinsons – Philadelphia put them to work. Large though the city was, it was not a totally foreign place. English was the default language of most of its citizens. There were unrelated Hutchinsons, the descendants of earlier immigrants from the north of England, scattered about its residential streets and even serving with distinction in its boardrooms. A famous travelling circus managed by Messrs Phineas T. Barnum, James Bailey and James Hutchinson had recently entertained Philadelphia. (James Hutchinson's share would be bought out for $650,000 by his partners a couple of years later, in 1887, allowing this particular Hutchinson to retire in unimaginable luxury and the show thereafter to tour simply as Barnum and Bailey's.)

Badly paid employment and basic lodgings were easily found. Philadelphia's tenements were notorious for their overcrowding – as many as 50 or 60 people sharing a single tenement terraced house, with a family to each room. Thirty or forty years earlier the city's workers had been among the most militant and revolutionary in America. But when the Hutchinsons arrived a devastating civil war had ended just 20 years earlier. The nation had still not healed itself; and it was engaged more with reconstruction and the benefits, however meagre to most working people, of a Golden Age of commercial expansion. Philadelphia was a calmer place in the 1880s than it had been in the 1840s. And besides, those English immigrants were – and perceived themselves as – birds of passage. America's industrial disputes were not yet their own. Philadelphia's filthy tenements were merely rest-stops on their road to a better life.

The Hutchinsons walked out of the riverside complex and into the town. They made their way past elegant colonial-Georgian townhouses and picturesque parks. They walked up broad boulevards lined with chestnut trees and those triumphant totems of white America: 100-foot-high telegraph poles weighted down like grapevines with countless clusters of packed conductor rods. They walked into the city centre through canyons of tall insurance buildings, trust companies, corporate headquarters, banks, hotels, real-estate brokers and savings and investment trusts.

They bought a copy of one of the local newspapers, the *Philadelphia Public Ledger*, and discovered an astonishing number and variety of situations vacant for both men and women. Philadelphia was in need of cooks and waiters, clerks and painters, laundresses and factory hands, carpenters, dressmakers, barbers, nurses, wallpaper hangers and people willing to earn a basic stipend by caring for other working citizens' vegetable gardens. Labourers were in demand throughout the city, from the wharves to the sensational edifice and tower of the enormous new City Hall, which had been begun in 1872 and was, like some medieval European cathedral, still in construction 13 years later. Earning a daily dollar in Philadelphia in 1885 would not be a problem. At the end of their first day they felt nervous, exhausted and exhilarated. They were facing a terrifying freedom.

It was of particular significance to the Hutchinsons that the local newspapers also carried large advertisements from gentlemen offering cures for most afflictions. Aware of the bad reputation which had attached to others of his kind, Professor Munyon of Arch Street announced that: 'There is no punishment too severe

. . . for those who deceive or take advantage of the sick. You may sell a shoddy garment for pure wool, and you only affect a man's purse, but when you palm off a spurious medicine on a sick person, you may cause months of suffering and possibly the loss of a precious life.'

Professor Munyon's conscience was clear. 'In this city alone more than thirty thousand people declare they have been cured by his little sugar pellets. Professor Munyon does not claim that his remedies will cure in every case, but he is prepared to prove that they do cure over 90 per cent of all curable cases where the remedies are taken according to directions.'

Sadly, Professor Munyon specialised chiefly in the cure of rheumatism, asthma, 'all Female complaints', kidney troubles, piles, consumption and neuralgia. His little sugar pellets and other pharmacological products were not designed to give sight to the blind.

But others were, and they found a ready market.

The remedies were many and various. Not long after Kate Wilkinson's arrival in the United States the Philadelphia newspapers would report the case of Thomas T. Hayden. Hayden was a celebrated actor on the north-east coast of America. In 1891 he was inexplicably – and apparently incurably – struck blind. Hayden's 50-year-old widowed mother consequently moved in to care for her son.

A year later, on the morning of 25 June 1892, Thomas Hayden woke up, got dressed and 'groped about the house' calling for his mother. Receiving no reply, he assumed that she had fainted. He got down on his hands and knees and crawled over every floor in the house, including the basement, until he finally discovered her dead of a heart attack before the kitchen stove.

Having buried his mother, Thomas Hayden determined to cure his own blindness. The actor placed himself in the hands of Augustus Theiss, a practitioner who promised to restore Hayden's vision within 12 months.

Theiss's treatment was painful and expensive, but plausible.

He had synthesised a liquid 'remedial agent' which would only work on a patient's eyesight if it was 'brought into close contact with the blood vessels'. So he had constructed a large wire brush bristling with 33 sharp steel prongs. Those prongs were placed against some exposed portion of Thomas Hayden's naked body. Augustus Theiss then 'by means of a spring, drives them into the flesh for an eighth of an inch or more, leaving 33 distinct punctures'. Theiss's remedial oil was rubbed into the holes, causing 'great pain for a few moments'.

After just two sessions with Augustus Theiss, Thomas Hayden was optimistic about regaining his sight despite – or perhaps because of – having been caused great pain. In the first treatment Theiss applied his steel brush to Hayden's body 421 times, causing around 14,000 punctures. On his second consultation Theiss upped the dose to 22,011 punctures (Hayden was presumably counting each one). With a total of more than 36,000 perforations in his body 'from head to foot', Thomas Hayden admitted to having 'suffered greatly, not so much from the prickings as from the rubbing of the oil into the skin, which is blistered by the operation'. The positive side was that Hayden felt such improved sensations in his body tone that he was confident of regaining his sight. Dr Theiss had assured him that after three months he would be able to 'distinguish forms', after six months 'to recognise friends, while at the end of the year recovery will be practically complete'.★

In fact, in the United States of America Kate Wilkinson and her family were spoiled for choice in their hunt for a cure. The secret of Augustus Theiss's 'remedial oil' may be found in the fact that 20 years earlier, in 1872, news had reached the USA of a German professor who had restored the sight of a blind naval

★ Thomas Hayden never did recover his sight. His acting career blighted, he nonetheless made himself available for recitations from memory at public events for the rest of the nineteenth century and into the twentieth, and took comfort – like many other performers of his time – from being a member of the fraternity named the Benevolent and Protective Order of Elks.

captain by injecting him in the armpit with strychnine. Strychnine being – 'as is well known' – a deadly poison, Professor Nagel of Tübingen used only modest quantities, reported the *New York Times*. But its effect on the myopic ship's captain was dramatic. 'On the fourth day of treatment, without help, he succeeded at midday in walking alone through the thoroughfares of the city to the home of his family, a mile from the infirmary.'

A cure for blindness presented obvious obstacles to its salesmen. Blindness was a cut-and-dried, black-and-white condition. A person was either blind or could see. Unlike maladies such as cancer, for which remedies were also enthusiastically advertised, it was difficult to peddle an alcohol-and-morphine-based alleviative for blindness and insist that the consequent short-term relief was the first step towards a full cure. Short-term relief for blindness was as elusive – and as difficult to feign – as a full cure. Most 'scientific' practitioners like Augustus Theiss therefore played a long game, warning that their remedies would take effect only gradually, over an unpredictable but extended period of months and years, so long as the patient continued to pay for the treatment.

There were, of course, exceptions. William Williams was imprisoned in Atlanta, Georgia, for swindling $2.50 from a blind man named Robert Ward. Williams had offered to cure Ward's blindness, on receipt of the $2.50, by hammering an iron tack into the back of his skull. Following the operation Ward remained blind and reported the fact to the Atlanta Police Department. The tack had not affected him much and had been removed, but the swindle, said Robert Ward, 'hurt considerable'.

Kate Wilkinson was no more likely to submit to iron tack treatment than she was prepared to rub the relics of saints on her sightless eyes. She and her family had not travelled to the United States of America in search of the superstition and witch's brews which were plentiful back in Europe, but to discover the latest advances of nineteenth-century medical science. They had come specifically for the magneticon and other branches of electro-therapy.

Cutting-edge nineteenth-century medical treatment did not come cheap. The $2.50 which William Williams received from Robert Ward for driving a nail into his head was on the lowest rung of surgical fees, and $2.50 was not an insignificant sum. While Tom Wilkinson and Miles Hutchinson had no difficulty finding work in Philadelphia, they were unlikely to become wealthy. Their unskilled labouring jobs paid them around $12 a week. Christopher Hutchinson, who had travelled west to join the other men in Pittsburgh, was already earning more money in the coalfield. Casual home-based piecework sewing or knitting would have allowed Rosina and Kate to add a few extra dollars to the communal funds. But their weekly rental of just two barely furnished rooms cost no less than $3 a week. Fuel had to be bought, and although food was plentiful and cheap, it still had to be paid for. The streets of Philadelphia were paved with nickel, not gold.

Electro-therapy, magnetism or mesmerism had been gathering credibility as a panacea for half a century in the United States before Kate Wilkinson and her extended family arrived. It was rooted in the belief that the human body was essentially vitalised by 'animal electricity'. If a part of that body malfunctioned, therefore, an artfully applied electrical current was the logical way to correct it. There were 'electro-vital forces' in the human physique, argued the qualified Chicagoan physician E. J. Fraser in 1863, which could be 'augmented or diminished at pleasure, by the application of artificial electricity'.

By the 1880s, commercial companies were marketing the battery-powered machines to apply that electricity to patients. A practitioner would stump up $25 for the battery, $10–$18 for the appliance and as much as $100 for an internal surgery galvano-cauteriser. Manuals came with the equipment. They said that the shocks imparted to patients by electro-therapeutics could stimulate digestion, calm nerves, remove moles, ulcers and tumours, correct sexual dysfunction . . . and restore eyesight.

No licence or qualifications were required by electrotherapists in the 1880s. Later in the century the American Graduated Nurses' Protective Association would campaign for federal legislation to ensure 'that no person shall practice electrotherapy, hydro-therapy or mechanico-therapy without holding a duly registered license as a trained nurse', but until then it was an open shop. And in the meantime, according to one authority, the efforts of qualified physicians 'to compete with irregular electrotherapists were actually counterproductive. By offering the technique in their own practices, they legitimised portable electric health machines that could easily be purchased by unlicensed practitioners . . .'

A stranger in a strange land, Kate Wilkinson would have put herself in the hands of a competent or a charlatan without knowing the difference. In fact, there was not much difference. In the United States in the 1880s qualified graduates of medical schools and unqualified miracle healers shared several identical debts to electro-therapy, the chief one being to recoup their $140 investment in the equipment.

That imperative resulted in medical charges – even in such a competitive environment as Philadelphia, which was pullulating with physicians – that the Wilkinsons and the Hutchinsons could not easily afford. Casual labouring in Philadelphia offered them no great prospects. The booming coalmining industry of western Pennsylvania, whose output would in just a few years outstrip even that of the Tyne and Wear field, offered both progress and regress.

It would be a step forward – possibly a large step forward – in potential financial reward. It would be a step backwards into the dark and dangerous world that the men had left behind in Britain. And although they did not know it, it would take them into the arenas of industrial disputes more violent and bitter than any which echoed around the collieries back home at Billy Row and Cornsay.

But they went. After those frustrating weeks of getting by and making do in Philadelphia, a consensus was reached. They would pack their things once more and travel to join their relatives in Pittsburgh.

I never went down a mine. British coalminers, and probably coalminers everywhere else, had a mildly schizophrenic attitude to their vocation. Defensive of it to the very last, proud of the solidarity of their comrades and the integrity of their communities, determined in the dignity of their calling, graciously receptive of their unrequested roles as both the commanding officers and the frontline troops of the working classes – most coalminers would nevertheless move as much earth aboveground as they ever did below to try to ensure that their sons did not have to follow them into the pit-cage.

Most failed, of course. During the hundred-year heyday of the British coal industry, between the middle of the nineteenth and the middle of the twentieth centuries, coalmining was as much a hereditary activity as was marquetry or membership of the House of Lords. Only a few got out. My father, William Hutchinson's youngest child and only son, was one of them. The scholarship which he won to grammar school broke one small circle and unlocked the gate of the cage for his children and theirs. The great majority of his fellow twentieth-century British miners' sons had the gate slammed in their faces 50 years later. Theirs was the humiliation of leaving the darkest of industrial jobs not on their own terms, but because after the sacrifice of generations and the supposedly unqualified esteem of their fellow citizens, they were considered to be unprofitable.

Then, in the 1980s and 1990s, coalminers and the sons of coalminers began to move. But fallacies about the geographical and social stasis of the earlier, Victorian British lower classes have become established. Received wisdoms have suggested that before the dynamic late-twentieth-century men and women – particularly impoverished men and women – lived a tribal life, were born and bred, married and died within the same fixed community.

Many did, and many still do. In 2008 no fewer than one third of all Britons were still living within five miles of their birthplace. The fraction of stabilised citizens could have been greater in the nineteenth century, even during the upheavals of the industrial revolution and the epochal exodus from the countryside to the cities and the manufacturing towns.

But what evidence we have suggests that it was not much greater, that the British working class was even then vastly more socially and geographically adventurous than our Christmas card images – and preferred folk memories – of timeless, frozen hamlets imply.

Jason Long of Colby College in Massachusetts has spent the days and weeks in dusty archives necessary to establish the precise statistics of Victorian British class mobility; to answering the question, did they stay or did they go? Professor Long concludes that they went – 'the British populace of the nineteenth century was highly mobile . . . Nineteenth-century Britain saw both high rates of internal mobility and overseas emigration'.

In the 30 years between 1851 and 1881, fully one quarter of Britons moved from one county to another. During the same period more than half of them changed their town or village of residence. That is not quite the twenty-first-century total of a transitory two thirds of the citizenry, but it is not very far away. It is recognisably close.

In my own adult life I have lived in six postal codes 600 miles apart. Compared to Miles and Rosina Hutchinson, my Victorian great-grandparents, I am a couch potato. In their 20s and 30s they lived in at least eight different places. Four thousand miles lay between the easternmost and the furthest west of their homes. Our journeys have been neither fully representative nor wholly exceptional of our classes and our centuries. That's the way that people were and people are – different.

2

Between the Sea and the Soil

Philadelphia, County Durham, 1821

> 'If ony, then, of Blacky's race
> Ha'e harder cairds than words te play,
> Wey then, poor dogs, ower hard's their case,
> And truth's in what wor preachers say.'
> – *Thomas Wilson, 'The Pitman's Pay' (1843)*

For the best and most obvious of reasons, there have never been photographs of Philadelphia in 1821 – just as none survive of Elizabeth, Rosina's mother, who was born there in that year. But from sketches and memories and contemporary written descriptions, we can piece together an image of the place.

Compared with what it was to become, Philadelphia in 1821 was rural, tranquil and small. To its east lay the open sea. To its north, south and west a pretty countryside of streams and rivers, cultivated fields and grazing meadows rubbed up against virgin woodland. Philadelphia sat at first slightly uneasily in those surroundings. It was not an ancient, organic parish of wattle and thatch. Philadelphia was a new town of stone, brick and slate. It was a planned model settlement. It had been created, and christened, in broken Greek, 'the Place of Brotherly Love' by its optimistic English founder, in the hope that its name could thereafter influence its character.

Its people, when Elizabeth was young, had a variety of early-nineteenth-century occupations. They were blacksmiths, stonemasons, wheelwrights, mill workers and schoolmistresses. They were publicans, glass-makers and agricultural labourers. They were shopkeepers, servants, nightwatchmen and joiners. As

Elizabeth grew into a young woman and the nineteenth century picked up speed, some Philadelphians were even employed as railway engineers.

But mostly, by a huge majority, the men were coalminers, the women were the daughters, wives and mothers of coalminers, and the children of Philadelphia were to be what their parents had been. Philadelphia was a colliery village in the north-eastern corner of England, five miles south-west of the port of Sunderland in County Durham. Elizabeth herself would never see the other, larger, more widely celebrated Philadelphia, at the far side of the North Atlantic Ocean. But four of her children would.

Elizabeth's Philadelphia was built on top of what was known, after its great rivers, as the Tyne and Wear coalfield. This vast resource would remain for two further centuries one of the biggest exploited deposits of coal in Europe. Coal had been harvested from the sea and the land in these parts for perhaps two millennia before the 1690s and 1700s, when Lord Scarborough decided to exploit this particular seam commercially.

By 1727 Scarborough had three underground pits operating in the earth below what was to become Philadelphia. Seven years later, in 1734, he sold his increasingly profitable lease to a partnership dominated by the wealthy Sunderland entrepreneur John Nesham. In 1774 Nesham sank a large and ambitious shaft from the surface to the main coal seam five miles south-west of Sunderland, in the central, Durham section of the field. The usual shacks, shelters, shanties, workshops and eventually rows of residential cottages grew up around this venture. Rather than let his colony on the industrial frontier adopt a second-hand name, John Nesham christened it himself. He called it Philadelphia. Nesham had a fondness for American references. Two years later he christened another Durham colliery Bunker Hill, after the bloody American War of Independence battle in 1775.

When Elizabeth was born in Philadelphia in 1821 it was a compact, dedicated colliery village. Nesham had sunk more pits on the same site, which he called after his daughters. Generations of nineteenth- and twentieth-century Philadelphia miners, including Elizabeth's father, would know the Dorothea and Elizabeth pits in a familiar diminutive, as the Dolly and the Betty. In the first decades of the nineteenth century there was living in Philadelphia a disproportionate number of girls and young women named Elizabeth and Dorothy. The possibility is not to be discounted that Elizabeth's collier father christened his own eldest daughter after the pit shaft down which he worked.

Elizabeth was raised in a placid, bucolic environment. The dirt and squalor of coal-mining districts was mostly, by definition, beneath the surface of the earth. Her father walked each day through coppices and green fields to a nearby pithead and laboured underground for ten or twelve hours each twenty-four, on a fore-shift (night-time until late morning) or a back-shift (morning until evening), every day of the week but the Sabbath, to earn the money to keep his family alive. The effect on his health and appearance of his long career underground – allied with an impoverished diet – was sadly apparent. The early-nineteenth-century pitman was described by a sympathetic witness as 'being diminutive in stature, misshapen and disproportionate in figure, with bowed legs and protruding chest. His features were equally unprepossessing, hollow cheeks, over-hanging brow, forehead low and retreating.'

His average life expectancy at birth was not much more than 30 years. The national British working class average life expectancy in the first half of the nineteenth century was not significantly older. Coalminers fell just short of the mean, due to lung and respiratory diseases, crippling individual accidents and pit disasters. The latter were frequent and savage.

But if the pitman's life was often short, it would be wrong to dismiss it as unrelievedly nasty and brutal. Thomas Wilson was born on the Durham bank of the River Tyne in 1773. He worked in coal mines as a boy, but in his leisure hours he studied. In his 20s, instead of hewing at the coal-face, he became a schoolteacher. In his 30s he became a partner in a profitable Tyneside business. A prodigious autodidact and early exemplar of the miner's urge for self-improvement, Wilson devoted much of his adult life to literature. In the late 1820s he wrote and published an epic dialect poem titled 'The Pitman's Pay'. Nominally about the activities of north-eastern miners on their fortnightly pay-nights, 'The Pitman's Pay' provides a sharp first-hand insight into the extramural activities of the early-nineteenth-century Durham miner.

It is faintly Hogarthian. There is no doubt that – on at least this one Saturday night every fourteen days – many if not most male miners got drunk and gambled. Some, although apparently a small minority even in the late-Georgian and Regency years, were devoted to betting 'On cock-fight, dog-fight, cuddy-race, / Or pitch-and-toss, trippet-and-coit . . .'. But following the first few pints, according to Wilson, the loosened tongues of the Saturday night majority would discuss much more than 'their wives and wark'. Wide-ranging debates around the inn tables would cover 'The famous feats done in their youth, / At bowling, ball, and clubby-shaw – / Camp-meetings, Ranters, Gospel-truth, / Religion, politics, and law.'

'Religion, politics, and law . . .' These men and women were far from being stupid or incurious, unambitious or disorganised people. As early as 1831 a Durham miner named Thomas Hepburn, who had worked underground since the age of eight, established the first Northern Union of Pitmen. This seminal association immediately attracted tens of thousands of Tyne and Wear miners to strike meetings, and a two-month walk-out achieved some concessions in hours and working conditions.

The clash of articulated opinions on a variety of elevated subjects hums down from those precious, lubricated Saturday nights of leisure. 'We need not wonder at the clatter, / When ev'ry tongue wags – wrong or right.'

If that was the life of Elizabeth's father, and the life of her other male relatives, Elizabeth herself was fortunate not to share it. The employment in underground pits of women (and boys under the age of ten) was not outlawed until the passage in 1842, when she was 21 years old, of the Mines and Collieries Act. In fact, most women in the mining communities of the Durham coalfield had not worked underground since the 1780s. Their husbands and fathers and, it must be presumed, several of the coalowners preferred them when possible to lead a domestic life above ground – a discrimination which was approved by almost all of the women themselves.

At the age of 21, Elizabeth escaped into marriage. Naturally, she married a coalminer. William Robson had been born a year before Elizabeth, in the parish of Washington, another County Durham pit-village nomenclaturally twinned with the United States of America. Washington stood ten miles west of Sunderland and five miles north of Philadelphia. In his teens William had moved with his father and mother a short distance south to live at Shiney Row in the northern outskirts of Philadelphia. Upon the 22-year-old William's marriage to the 21-year-old Elizabeth in 1842, he was working in the Success pit at Philadelphia, and William and Elizabeth set up home in what was then the Success Row of colliers' cottages.

This couple's marriage would endure for more than 50 years: an almost miraculous span for an industrial working-class partnership in the nineteenth century. It would also produce 11 children who survived into and beyond infancy. The youngest of the daughters was christened Rosina.

In her first five years of wedlock Elizabeth gave birth to three girls, one of whom was named after her. They were followed in 1850 by the senior boy, who took his father's name of William. William was pursued into and out of the family cradle between 1852 and 1864 by five more daughters. In 1864 and 1866 – when she was 43 and 45 years old – Elizabeth Robson's last two children were boys.

The eleven infants were born in five different places. As a hewer at the coal-face William Robson hawked his trade from pit to pit. Over 200 new coalmines were sunk in County Durham during the nineteenth century, so there was ample choice. The number of Durham mineworkers rose from 34,000 to 153,000 between 1844 and 1900. There was clearly work to be found – but even in this employee's market, between the smashing of Thomas Hepburn's Northern Union of Pitmen shortly after the 1831 strike and the growth of the Durham Miners' Union in the 1870s, it was work under the coal-owners' conditions.

For most of his life William Robson was employed under the 'bond' system. Bonded labour was his employers' solution to the problem posed to them by an excess of available jobs over willing workers in a free market. When he began adult employment as a teenager William Robson was bonded to one colliery for exactly a year. During those 12 months William was obliged to present himself as ready to work on every labouring day. The colliery owner, however, was not obliged to offer him work on that day, or to pay him if he was stood down. The coal-owner did not have to renew the 12-month bond, nor during its enforcement was he obliged to give William any form of continuous employment. If William Robson or any of his colleagues were laid off during the period of the bond, they were not paid. But neither could they seek work elsewhere – they remained bonded to the Success or any other pit. Any miner who broke his bond was open to arrest, conviction, blacklisting and even deportation to Australia. Occasionally newspaper advertisements named and urged the forcible return of 'runaway' coalminers.

A Durham coalfield strike failed in 1844, when William Robson was 24 years old, newly married and with one small daughter. As a punishment for the dispute the coal-owners reduced the bond period from twelve months to one month. The 12-month bond was not reintroduced until 1864, 20 years later. It was not completely removed by government legislation until 1872, by which time William Robson was 52 years old and still working as a Durham coalminer.

When he was employed and paid, William and Elizabeth Robson were largely dependent for their household goods on the Tommy Shop, or the coal-owner's company store. Until the 1831 strike many miners had been paid entirely with tokens – 'Tommy checks' – for the Tommy Shop. Tommy Shops, given their corporate monopoly, were habitually overpriced (by as much as 40 per cent for cheese, 33 per cent for bacon and butter, and 45 per cent for tea, according to one Mining Commission report of 1843) and badly stocked – they seem to have marked their name on the English language in the disgusted expression 'tommy-rot'. The payment of a miner's entire wage in Tommy checks was supposedly abandoned by the coal-owners in 1831, but substantial part-payment, as well as the Tommy Shops themselves, persisted for decades. As no less a journalist than Karl Marx observed, in 1864 it was still common for British coalminers to be paid their wages, immediately after their hot, dry, fatiguing shift, inside the beer-dispensing Tommy Shop itself.

Elizabeth and William Robson lived for all of their long lives in tied pit cottages. Those terraced rows of basic colliery housing had been erected by the coal-owners to house whichever work-ers they had on bond in any particular month or year. The loss of bonded work meant an automatic loss of home. But the bond itself did not guarantee miners' housing. Strikers were routinely evicted, as – albeit less routinely, but with absolute authority – was any mining family which complained about its sanitation, weather-proofing or other conditions.

Elizabeth Robson's daughters and sons had known no other life. It varied only slightly in environment, and in the nature of their Methodist or Church of England hedge school, as their father shifted bond and work, and as their busy, cheerful, growing family traversed from one pit-cottage to the next. As William Robson moved from the Success pit in Philadelphia to a bond at Brandon Colliery seven miles away, and then to a bond in Brancepeth Colliery, a short walk from Brandon, so Elizabeth and his children moved from Success Row to No. 162 Brandon Colliery, to No. 5 Oakenshaw Row at Brancepeth.

By the late 1870s, when thanks to the 1872 legislation William had for the first time in his life an unbonded job at Burnhope Colliery – which was still within a seven-mile radius of both his and his wife's birthplaces in Washington and Philadelphia – only one girl, the one named Rosina, was left with her 60-year-old parents. The other seven surviving women had married and moved away.

William and Elizabeth Robson had experienced modest improvements during their six decades in the Tyne and Wear field. Angus Watson, a businessman who was born in 1874 and raised within ten miles of the Robson family in the north Durham coalfield, would later recall the life and conditions of such late-Victorian collier families during his own – more privileged – boyhood. Their homes, Watson said,

> . . . often consisted of a 'but-and-ben' – that was a tiny cottage of two living rooms that were a kitchen and a bedroom, with a garret overhead where the children slept . . .
>
> In front of the cottages were the outhouses containing the earth closet and the supply of coal – provided as part of the colliers' earnings by the colliery – and behind, the little strip of garden where he cultivated the vegetables that his family would otherwise have had to do without.
>
> There rarely was any social centre in the village; the two places of meeting were the public-house and the chapel. The owners of the colliery and its management generally lived away from the district, as was natural, for there was little that was tolerable in the smoke and the noise of the colliery, and the all-pervasive odour of gas and fumes that hung like a pall over the village.

But their lives were not all dirt and death and industrial dispute. Angus Watson's boyhood colliers were as likely to attend chapel (trade union leaders were frequently also local lay preachers) and take a pledge of abstinence, as disappear into a mire of drink and debt.

> He [the collier] was generally a keen gardener, and took his place with great success in local exhibitions at the annual flower shows; he planned bowling matches with clubs from the surrounding villages; he had his greyhound, as well cared for as the wife or children, and engaged it in rabbit-coursing contests; he possessed

his prize pigeons, and flew these in competition with those of his neighbours.

'Those were the men and women,' the wealthy and successful Angus Watson would write 55 years later, '. . . whom I began to admire and respect as I gradually began to understand them. I saw them under many aspects: they were involved in one of the long coal-strikes of the '80s. They faced the peril with quiet courage and resultion . . . Their example has meant much to me as I look back on my life's journey, and realise all that I learned from them.'

In 1881 the pit-cottage named No. 27 Burnhope Colliery was home to the 61- and 60-year-old William and Elizabeth Robson, their youngest son, the 15-year-old Thomas, who was working with his father in Burnhope Colliery, and one daughter. Seventeen-year-old Rosina, having left school, helped her mother at home. Despite 'the all-pervasive odour of gas and fumes', she still lived in part the rural life of her childhood. She collected wild berries and rhubarb in season. She will have shared with Angus Watson ten miles away the 'bright moonlit winter nights, when we skated on the "Gut" on the Willows . . . there were Guisers, when we blacked our faces and "dressed up", and sang carols at the doors of neighbours' houses. We possessed little lanterns, with red and green glasses, when we played "I spy light" as we hid in Week's Dene . . .'

Domestically, Rosina nurtured the hens in the yard. She worked on the vegetable patch. She cooked and preserved foods. She baked bread. She helped with the weekly wash every Monday, and she cleaned the rooms. She kept the fire in and heated the water for her father's and her brother's after-shift hip-baths (in which they would scrupulously clean every part of their bodies but their backs, which were left dirty for fear of weakening the spine).

The older daughters, Rosina's sisters, could have accepted most of those household chores, along with helping to raise the younger children, as a traditional and inevitable part of their lot. But Rosina was the youngest daughter; had been for seventeen years the baby of seven older sisters. The teenaged Rosina's attitude to helping her 60-year-old mother around the house was nuanced. Rosina was restless.

One by one, in the years since her infancy, she had watched her sisters marry and leave home. Ann, who was 21 years older, had done so before Rosina was even conceived. The others – Elizabeth, Margaret, Sarah, Mary and Rachel – had subsequently grown into adulthood and deserted her at regular intervals. At the very least Rosina anticipated, in some near future, the adventure of her own adult life. She visualised her own suitor and marriage and children and tied colliery home. She imagined an escape.

The matchings of four of her five older sisters were uncontroversial. Only Rachel, her senior by three years, had stepped slightly off the beaten marital path by marrying into an Irish family. Her husband, James McCormack, had been born in Durham in 1859, but his parents had earlier crossed the Irish Sea from their homeland during the famine years.

That did not make them immigrants in any but the most nationalist reading of the word. In the nineteenth century the whole of Ireland was a part of the United Kingdom, as Wales and Scotland and indeed Northern Ireland would continue to be throughout the twentieth century and into the twenty-first. They may have been in many quarters reluctant partners in the British enterprise, but in the 1850s, '60s, '70s and '80s, in the period of the McCormack family's upheaval, Irishmen and women were as fully UK citizens as was anybody born in Deptford, Dover or Durham. In crossing from Dublin to Liverpool to escape starvation, they were doing no more than transferring themselves from one region of their nation to another.

The McCormacks were part of a large and growing body of Irish people in the north-east of England, and they were chiefly distinguished from their neighbours and workmates not by their accents, but by their religion. The McCormacks were Roman Catholic in England; the immense struggles of 200 and 300 years earlier: the routed invasion attempt of the Spanish Armada, the Gunpowder Plot (whose ringleader was and still is burned in effigy each November by gleeful English children), the long and bloody death-struggle of the Stuart dynasty, had left deep impressions in the folk memories of ordinary English Protestants. Just 30 years before James McCormack was born to his Irish parents in County Durham no Roman Catholic of any nationality had been permitted to take a British parliamentary seat or was eligible for any other public office. The Tory government which in 1829 passed the Catholic Emancipation Act had then almost immediately been destroyed by widespread public disquiet and dissent among its own ranks. (One hundred and fifty years after James McCormack was born, it was still not legally permissible for anyone of his family's faith to become or to marry the monarch of Great Britain.)

But by the 1880s Irish families in the Tyne and Wear coalfield were far too numerous to be regarded as an impertinent minority. In 1881, two years after Rachel Robson married into an Irish family, there were in County Durham alone almost 37,000 people who had been born in Ireland and in the whole of the north-eastern coalfield almost 70,000 who were, like Rachel's husband James McCormack, of direct Irish descent. They amounted to 7 per cent of the total population. Their second and third generations – who all would speak in Tyneside and Wearside accents and dialects rather than the brogue of their parents – were too many to ignore or ostracise, even by those who might still have preferred to blackball Catholics. The Tyne and Wear Irish would not become so celebrated, so segregated or so assertive as their Hibernian cousins in Liverpool, Glasgow and London, but they were almost as plentiful.

If they were not yet completely assimilated, the McCormacks and their compatriots encountered fewer problems in the north-east than did the Irish elsewhere in England and Scotland. Apart from anything else, they found themselves immigrants in a region of other immigrants. The demands of the labour boom in the Tyne and Wear field meant that in 1881 one third of the population of County Durham, 100,000 out of 330,000 residents, had not been born there.

Those 100,000 incomers had travelled from all over the British Isles. They had journeyed for jobs from Scotland and Cornwall, from – as we shall see – the dying lead mines of Yorkshire, and from hungry Ireland. The nineteenth-century Durham countryside contained a multitude of hurriedly raised churches and missions of different denominations. The nineteenth-century Durham pit shafts and iron works were a Bedlam of dialects. The McCormack family were not therefore, as one author puts it, 'over-conspicuous'. Their Irish brogue and their Catholic faith were only one way of talking and one way of worshipping among many. In a kingdom of strangers, no one was really strange.

The fate of the marriage of Rachel and James McCormack would later bring consternation to this extended family. But in 1881 there was no sign of that. In 1881 young Rosina Robson's imagination would instead have worked overtime after the last sister to leave, Catherine, married a young coalminer named Tom Wilkinson. That was a wholly unexpected development. Neither Catherine nor her family had dared to hope for such a departure. Catherine was different. Catherine, who was known to her family as Kate, had throughout Rosina's childhood worked assiduously, mostly indoors, at whatever she was able to do. This had once involved caring as best as she was able for her two younger sisters. When they became old enough to take care of themselves, she had undertaken all or most of the family's knitting.

Few other tasks were easily available to her, for Kate had been born functionally blind. She could vaguely discern shape and colour, but little else.

The most likely cause of her disability is that her mother, Elizabeth, contracted German measles in the early stages of her pregnancy with Kate. Elizabeth would not have understood the danger to her unborn child – she may hardly have noticed the illness itself. German measles, or rubella, was in 1858 unrecogised as an affliction. Elizabeth would have suffered for two or three days from a mild fever and a rash, perhaps combined with occasional headaches. And then – almost before a busy mother and miner's wife had time to worry – it will have passed, leaving only fine flakes of skin from the disappearing rash fluttering from her face.

Neither Elizabeth Robson nor anybody else in 1858 knew that as many as 20 per cent of women who acquired German measles in the first trimester of pregnancy had subsequently a 40 per cent chance of delivering a baby with eye defects or total blindness. Elizabeth may have been among the 20 per cent; Kate among the unlucky 40 per cent. And just as there was no recognition of, let alone cure for, rubella, there was – in Britain at least – no known human answer to blindness.

Kate's prospects were poor. Most coalminers' children were not, in the 1860s, sent to school. And hardly anybody's sightless daughters were offered education of any kind. Not until 1893 would an Act of Parliament introduce the 'Compulsory Education of Blind and Deaf Children from five to sixteen years of age' in England and Wales. There was in Britain a small handful of asylums whose chief purpose was to teach the blind a trade, but none of them was in the vicinity of County Durham. It was broadly accepted that only a few professions were open to blind men, most obviously those of taking Holy Orders, entering the law, offering massages, piano-tuning and musical performance. Of those five, only massage and musical performance were feasible careers for naturally gifted blind women, and the young Kate Robson was no more likely to have the opportunity to discover whether or not she was a gifted musician than to be permitted by her parents to train as a masseuse.

Kate Robson's list of nineteenth-century role-models was short. A roster of exemplary blind people which was devised by W. H. Illingworth, superintendent of Henshaw's Blind Asylum in Manchester, included just three women. Two of them were the celebrated and exceptional American blind and deaf test cases Laura Bridgeman and Helen Keller. The other was Elizabeth Gilbert, the daughter of the Bishop of Chichester, who in 1854 started a workshop for blind people in London.

Kate's father, William, was neither American nor the Bishop of Chichester. And if Kate Robson ever studied the lives of her three famous contemporaries, one commonplace would have been obvious to her. Laura Bridgeman, Helen Keller and Elizabeth Gilbert never married or had children.

The first – if it was marriage to a sighted man – was acceptable, the second was not. But without the prospect of offspring a nineteenth-century husband would be difficult to attract. We know little of the personal thoughts and hidden ambitions of British blind women at that time. Earlier in the century in France, where the treatment of blind people was more advanced, an educated young blind woman named Therese-Adele Husson applied for lodging and financial assistance to the Royal Hospice of the Quinze-Vingts in Paris.

Part of Husson's written application to the hospice was later published as *Reflections: The Life and Writings of a Young Blind Woman in Post-Revolutionary France*. In it she expressed the firm opinions that blind men should never marry blind women, that blind women should never marry at all, and that (consequentially) blind women should never aspire to have children. Therese-Adele Husson then served as a personal paradigm of those strictures, by breaking each one of them. She married a blind man, had two children – and then died at the age of 28 in a house fire from which her sightless husband was unable to save her.

Kate Robson would not have known of Therese-Adele Husson, but she would have understood her precepts. Only the support and affection – which would be largely unconditional – of her family and her community would in any normal life offer the little blind girl her chance of happiness. Escape and adventure seemed, to Kate Robson and her parents and her sisters, to be off the agenda.

Then in 1879, when she was 21 years old, the 23-year-old local coalminer Tom Wilkinson happened along and suggested a form of normality by whisking her off to a marital bed five miles away at Stone Row, the pit cottages of Twizell Colliery.

And her life would subsequently be very far from normal. The blindness which could have entombed it would in fact release it, and would – with the help of other extraordinary phenomena – extend beyond any expectation the boundaries of her family.

On the desk beside me is a buffalo nickel. It is a family heirloom – aside from a coalminer's build, possibly the only legacy which has been handed down over three generations of the male side of my family. I used to think that we did not go back in recorded history much further than that, until I discovered otherwise.

It is a beautiful and also an intriguing old coin, partly because my grandfather had, as a boy, held it in his grubby palm. It is a five-cent piece with the date worn and obscured. On one side (heads?) is the bas-relief profile of an Indian brave, Roman-nosed, with two feathers hanging jauntily from his crop, and the single word 'Liberty'. On the other (tails?) is a terrific bison, crouched as though prepared to charge or flee, circumscribed with the legend: 'United States of America, E Pluribus Unum'. The Latin tag means 'Out of many, one'.

My grandfather gave that nickel to my father. My father gave it to me. Before his death I persuaded him to write in a reporter's notebook his second-hand recollections of the family provenance of the buffalo nickel. My father's memory and handwriting were both deteriorating in 1995, but that notebook also lies on the desk beside me.

He wrote of his own grandparents, father, uncles and aunts, with the thick black schoolteacher's fountain pen that he would never relinquish for a ballpoint or typewriter, let alone a computer keyboard: '1883 – USA (Pittsburgh). Miles Hutchinson Rosina. Great-aunt Kate (the knitter), blind, but sense of taste, touch etc. Children – William, John, Tom, Rosina, Miles, ?, ?, Alice, Cath, Fred. ? ? others.'

So they had, they really had been there. They had stayed there, died there and been born there.

When my father made those notes I had recently returned from the Ionian island of Ithaca. There is some academic dispute about whether or not contemporary Ithaca is the Ithaca to which, Homer told us, Odysseus returned after 20 busy years warring in Troy and making his way home. I had mentioned this debate to a schoolteacher in the small Ithacan village of Stavros. He smiled, and produced from a drawer a Bronze Age priest's headband which had, he said, been recovered from a cave in the cliffs below. Inscribed on the headband in perfectly legible Cyrillic were the words: 'Dedicated To King Odysseus'.

Comparisons between Odysseus and my grandfather would on the whole be odious. William Hutchinson was not nearly so fond of telling improbable stories of his own expedition. And it must be allowed that a buffalo nickel and a few scrawled sentences in a notepad do not carry the same archaeological weight as a Bronze Age relic in Ithaca. But they were each, in a minor and momentous way, that rarest of things: the literal confirmation of mythology.

Tales of Ordinary Freedom

Thwaite, North Yorkshire, 1858

'An' there's Skewdale, lad . . . Champion, isn't it?'

The valley, steep-sided in the main, rose in three great terraces opposite. This immense land mass, upon which slowly-moving cloud shadows continuously varied the prevailing tones of green, purple and brown, climbed to a far-extending summit . . .

– *Thomas Armstrong,* Adam Brunskill *(1952)*

While Elizabeth Robson was giving birth to her blind baby Kate in the summer of 1858, 40 miles away, a long day's hike to the south-west of Brandon Colliery, a two-year-old boy was learning to walk through the rough lanes of a tiny hamlet lost in the North Yorkshire Dales.

Miles Hutchinson had never known a world much beyond the huddled greystone cottages of Thwaite. People walked and carts were hauled down the paved track of Cloggerby Rigg, on the route from the market towns of Kirkby Stephen in the west to Reeth in the east, through the outskirts of Thwaite, but little Thwaite detained them not at all. Travellers and traders entered the margins of the village, crossed the humped-back bridge that spanned a bubbling tributary of the River Swale, and were gone again in minutes.

From all the narrow sides of Thwaite the immense bare shoulders of Swaledale rose towards the sky, enveloping and diminishing the modest settlement at their feet. Miles's miniature universe of village lanes, meadows, river and bridge was circumscribed by those hills, but they also represented an intriguing future, which became with each infant birthday steadily more comprehensible. On most of the mornings since Miles Hutch-inson had been born in November 1855, his father and other men of Thwaite had climbed the hills, to earn at least part of their living mining for lead.

Miners they all were, but the people who dug lead in Swaledale were different from those who cut coal in County Durham. They were different in conditions of work and quality of life, different in tradition and history, different perhaps in character and different certainly in expectation. The nineteenth-century Durham mining community was mostly new, transient and volatile. The Swaledale mining community had been at work in its lonely valleys for at least 1,000 years. The colliery village of Philadelphia in County Durham was created and named by an industrialist as recently as the 1770s. The name of Thwaite means a piece of claimed agricultural land and probably originated before the Norman Conquest, in the Anglo-Saxon word 'thweoten' – 'to clear away trees'.

The work itself was different. Some lead mining took place underground (although never so far underground as the Betty and Dolly shafts at Philadelphia), but much of it was done in the open air. Seams of lead were traditionally exposed at the surface by 'hushing', which was the sudden release of a dammed stream down a hill-top vale, causing a flash-flood which stripped away the top-soil and exposed the mineral deposits. Those deposits were then hacked out of the ground like tree-stumps, by men who knew all about removing tree-stumps, and carted off to the nearby smelt. Nobody in any age would describe nineteenth-century lead mining as an enviable occupation. But there were worse jobs to be found, a few dozen miles away. Compared with the bonded labour of the Durham mining community, the Swaledale miners had better terms of employment and far more independence. Swaledale lead miners were often settled agriculturalists with their own homes, small-holdings and stock. Miles Hutchinson's great-uncle, William Hutchinson, proudly declared to the national census enumerators that he was occupied both as a lead miner and a farmer. Not as a farm labourer, but as a farmer – an important distinction.

Most of the working families of Swaledale could not, however, have survived there without the lead.

Two miles down the dale from Thwaite – invisible among folds in the escarpment, but a mere half-hour's walk away – stood the much larger settlement of Muker. Thwaite looked to Muker: to its school, to its shops, to its church, to its market and its fair. Many a Thwaite person would, in future life, describe themselves actually as hailing from the parish of Muker. People had heard of Muker; no one had heard of Thwaite. Miles Hutchinson may not, as a boy, have known much of the world outside Thwaite, but he certainly did know the bustling streets of Muker.

In the spring of 1855, 25-year-old lead miner John Hutchinson married 20-year-old Alice Alderson, the daughter of another Thwaite family. It was therefore as the son of a lead miner that Miles Hutchinson was born in November that year. Not for another five years would Alice Hutchinson raise a child past infancy. To John and Alice Hutchinson, Miles would have been a treasured asset. His young brother Thomas came along in 1860, and at first Thomas also seemed likely to escape the lethal ambushes of a nineteenth-century babyhood.

Six years passed between John and Alice's country wedding in 1855 and the spring day in 1861 when the national census enumerators arrived, with their pens and ink and official forms, to record this young family in its stone cottage in the isolated Swaledale hamlet of Thwaite. Those six years were both professionally and personally a period of unusual calm and security in the troubled life of John Hutchinson, and consequently of his oldest son Miles. There followed two decades of death, redundancy and loss.

Their 26-year-old wife and mother Alice may already have been mortally ill when those census enumerators called. Her death certificate recorded that she had been unwell for six weeks when she died, in the presence of her husband John, on 19 May

1861. She had suffered from a 'disease of the brain'. She could have had a stroke, and lingered on for over a month. Or she may have had a tumour that manifested in its later stages as epilepsy or blindness. An infection may have 'gone to the brain', causing encephalitis . . .

Eighteen months later Alice was followed to the graveyard by her two-year-old son Thomas, who died of pneumonia in the relentlessly wet October of 1862, in the arms of a childless middle-aged neighbour called Margaret Kearton. The cottage at No. 68 Thwaite was suddenly a quiet and empty place. At the age of 32 John Hutchinson was a widower and single parent. At the age of six Miles Hutchinson had lost, within a year-and-a-half, his mother and his younger brother. The lead miner and his son were alone.

That was not only regrettable; it was, in 1862, an unsustainable situation. The six-year-old Miles did not attend school – in adulthood he was incapable of writing his own name. He could not be watched over and fed by kindly neighbours while his father worked for each and every day of the remaining six, seven or eight years of his childhood, even in the friendly lanes and fields of Thwaite. And at the age of 32, John Hutchinson was quite young enough to attract another bride.

He did so within eight months. John Hutchinson met, and married in May 1863, a 25-year-old woman from Wensleydale, the next glacial valley south of Swaledale. Ellen Routh had been born in Aysgarth and was working as a servant for a manufacturer in Hawes when John swooped to carry her north, over the high watershed to Thwaite.

Ellen lived for only another year. In September 1864 she died while giving birth to a son. This infant survived, and was named Christopher. As he buried his second spouse in two years, John Hutchinson, his troubles doubled, may have despaired of his ability to keep a wife alive. Eight-year-old Miles Hutchinson could be forgiven for concluding that mothers were a transient blessing.

This battered family of three males faced another threat, of which only John Hutchinson might have been fully aware. He stood likely to lose his job.

The lead mines and smelts of upper Swaledale had been in serious decline for 40 years. Their contribution to the new industrial British economy had peaked in the 1820s. Cheaper imports from abroad, chiefly from Spain, had since the end of the Napoleonic Wars steadily undercut the industry. The danger was alarming as early as 1830, when the people of Arkengarthdale sent a 'Petition against Importation of Lead' to the House of Commons. The petitioners begged leave 'to represent to the House, that in their humble opinion the present distress of that and other mining districts is much increased by the almost unrestricted importation of Lead and Lead Ore; and praying the House to take the distressed situation of that parish into consideration, and grant such relief either by imposing a sufficient protecting Duty upon Foreign Lead and Lead Ore, or by such other means as the House may think proper.'

Their plea went unanswered. No duty was imposed on Spanish lead. By the 1860s there was evidence before John Hutchinson's eyes that the decline might be worse than serious. It could be terminal. Shafts had been closing, and men made unemployed, at a steady rate throughout the 1840s and 1850s. Lead miners' earnings had in some cases halved in 30 years. The population of Muker had fallen from almost 1,500 in the 1820s to less than a thousand in the 1860s.

Throughout his youth and early married life, John Hutchinson had watched his neighbours leave. Some decided to join what they could not beat, and went to work the fertile lead mines near Granada in southern Spain.*

Some went to lead mines elsewhere in Britain. Some mined other minerals and fossil fuels in other parts of Britain. And a

---

* The only substantial work of fiction based on the lead mining industry in the Yorkshire Dales, *Adam Brunskill* by Thomas Armstrong, is set in the early 1880s. When the young Adam Brunskill returns to the land of his father, back home in 'Skewdale', the villages are almost as silent and empty as the mine shafts and smelts.

great number went from Swaledale across the Girt Dub, as they called the Atlantic Ocean, to the United States of America.

Both John and Miles Hutchinson were accustomed in Thwaite and Muker to stories and rumours of new lives in the New World. In 1839, when John had been nine years old, William Harker Calvert had left Thwaite for the American mid-west in the company of ten other local men, all of whom pledged to stick together until they reached their destination. Calvert's band was not the last.

Many of them went to Dubuque, west of the Mississippi River, where rich veins of lead had been uncovered and mined. There, in places such as English Hollow on the Fever River, they settled in the land of promise.

'We have no crown,' wrote Jonathan Alderson from the Fever River to his relatives back in Arkengarthdale, 'no duty, no bishops, nor yet have I seen a beggar running from door to door nor anything like an overseer gathering rates. We sit in our humble little cot free of rent, we can turn on the prairie horses or cows free and, by humbly asking leave to mow, we can have as much hay as we please. No gamekeepers, we work as we please, we play when we please, we have no Stuarts to bow to, one is as independent as another but we never forget our native land.'

Those were tempting tales of ordinary freedom. They were leavened with such exotica as the legend of John Harker from Muker, who made his way to the republic of Colombia in South America, married a glamorous young Colombiana named Mercedes Mutis and became director of the Zipaquira lead mines. (John Harker never returned, but his grandson Simon was sent from Colombia in the 1880s to be educated at a Catholic college in the north of England.)

While John Harker found a wife in South America, the North American dalesmen were generally less lucky. There was an insufficiency of eligible young women on the banks of the Fever

River. So in 1848, after nine years in the Mississippi basin, William Harker Calvert returned to Thwaite with money in his pocket. He married Jane Alton in Muker Parish Church and in 1849 the couple sailed back to New Orleans and took a Mississippi steamboat up to Fever River, where they proceeded to enjoy a long and distinguished life as stalwarts of the pioneer community.

John Hutchinson was 19 years old, single and working as an underpaid lead miner when William Calvert returned to Thwaite to display his prosperity, win his girl and whisk her back across the Atlantic Ocean to a place without crowned heads, taxes, bishops or gamekeepers.

When his second wife, Ellen, died in 1863, leaving him with two young sons, John was working the seam on Kisdon Hill, a mile above Thwaite. He was an employee of the Kisdon Mining Company, which worked its way through ever more unproductive veins of lead before stuttering towards closure in the late 1860s and finally suspending operations in 1870.

Having lost two wives and a son, in his late 30s John Hutchinson also lost his job. He was left with few alternatives. He packed his things, prepared his sons and left Thwaite for the last time. He moved over the county border into Durham, and took a 12-month bond at a coal mine in the Tyne and Wear Field.

Given his longer working day, more hazardous conditions and crowded industrial environment, it was even more unthinkable for a Durham coalminer's than a Thwaite lead miner's children to have no mother. John Hutchinson remarried almost immediately. Louisa Mole was the 19-year-old daughter of a carpet-weaver when she took her vows with the 36-year-old John at the registry office in Auckland, County Durham, in March 1869. Within nine years she had presented him with three more sons and two daughters. They would all survive. As much to the point, so would she.

In 1869 John and Louisa Hutchinson, Miles and Christopher set up home in a colliery cottage in Billy Row, a small Durham mining village a short walk north of the township of Crook. Almost immediately, the teenaged Miles followed his father down the Lucy pit of Pease's West Colliery at Billy Row. And almost immediately after that, the cottage at Crook-with-Billy-Row grew too small to contain the third family of John Hutchinson. In 1870 and 1871, the birth of Fred was quickly followed by the arrival of young John. In 1873 baby Hannah was born. William appeared in 1875. It was time for the 19-year-old Miles to strike out on his own.

He had grown into a handsome adult. Miles Hutchinson was of medium height – perhaps slightly taller than the average nineteenth-century coalminer. He was lean and muscular and rangy, with an erect stance and a head of rich black hair. His face was proud and stubborn; his nose was straight, his chin was firm, and his eyes – above all, his eyes – commanded attention. Dark and deepset, they gazed steadily, uncompromisingly, fixedly out from beneath a stern brow. They were the unblinking eyes of a poker professional or a gunhand. If they did not belong to a man who was unafraid of whatever life or death might bring, they did belong to a man who was determined to stare down a dangerous world.

Miles took with him out of Billy Row his 11-year-old brother Christopher, his remaining human connection with his abandoned rustic childhood. Miles and Christopher, two strong young men like so many others from the rural hinterlands, moved tracklessly through the seething central Durham coalfield. They climbed the steep terraced main street of Billy Row, strode by the village's pasturelands and walked for half a dozen miles due north across the high moor before descending to the recently opened pit at Cornsay Colliery. They took lodgings there with an aging coalminer and began their independent adult working lives underground.

In 1879, their father John Hutchinson died of a 'suffocating virus'. He was 49 years old. He had outlived two wives and been survived by a third. It was the turn of Louisa and her five young children to be left alone. Her 69-year-old widowed mother, Jane

Mole, moved into the Billy Row cottage to help with her daughter's fatherless family.

For their part, six miles away at Cornsay Colliery, at the ages of 23 and 15 years, Miles and Christopher had lost their last blood link to Thwaite and the farming, smithing, lead mining Hutchinsons of Swaledale.

One thing that I thought I knew with absolute certainty about the male side, the Hutchinson side, of my family was that they were Tynesiders. As their nineteenth-century connections with central County Durham emerged during the research of this book, and some of that Tyneside soil began to feel unstable, I mentioned my uncertainty to a rooted cousin. They hadn't been Tynesiders after all, I suggested hesitantly. They had been Mackems. No, no, no, she replied. They were Geordies. Full on, proper Geordies, every one of them.

In our lifetimes they were, but not before. That is important only because of their accents.

On reflection, delete the word 'only'. The way that Miles and Rosina and Kate and Tom spoke is of unqualified importance, and they did not talk like Geordies. That fact, tedious and baffling outside the north-east of England, is inflammatory between Crook and Morpeth. We can also presume that it will assist with our realisation of these characters if we know that when they wished to tell someone, 'Come on, don't take that' they said 'Ha'way, dinnit tak that' instead of 'Howay, divint tyek tha'.

It is down to the Vikings. When, a millennium before Miles and Rosina lived there, they sailed up the River Tyne and settled on its banks, they deposited large and abrasive fragments of their dialect. 'We say "gang oot" for "go out",' a proud Geordie uncle once told me. 'In Norwegian cinemas the "Way Out" sign says "Oot Gang" . . .' (In fact it more usually says 'Exit', and the Norsemen who colonised the east coast of England were mostly from modern Denmark. But he was essentially right: the classical Norse for 'way out' is 'utgang', and the Danish is 'udgang'.)

On the immediate north and south banks of the Tyne such loan-words and loan-phrases, while never supplanting Early English, buried *themselves deep into the local lexicon. But as the river drifted out of sight and mind their influence, while still present, gradually diluted and merged into the gentler brogues of rural northern England. In the eighteenth and nineteenth centuries they also absorbed the throaty 'pitmatic' accent and mineworking vocabulary of the Tyne and Wear collieries. It was a slow and polite mode of expression. Even its most intimate obscurities were, to any sympathetic outsider, both charming and quickly comprehensible. This was the easy, rolling dialect of the Robson sisters and of all of their husbands but one.*

The exception was Miles Hutchinson. Just as a spoken accent is dictated by peer rather than by parental influence, so it is usually established by a person's early teens. Miles Hutchinson spent his formative years in another phonetic world from County Durham. He will never have lost the sound of Swaledale. Where his wife said 'thee' and 'thou' Miles will have satisfied himself with 'tha' or merely 't''. When Miles said to her (something like), 'Rosina, pet, we mun pack and gow t' Pittsberg', Rosina will have conveyed to her sister (something like), 'Kyate, hinny, we'll hev te pack an gan te Pittsborg.'

They will, however, all have agreed with the same word. 'Aye.'

4

Sisters

Billy Row, County Durham, 1882

If, as sometimes happened [in the 1880s], a girl had to be married in haste, she was thought none the worse of on that account. She had secured her man. All was well. ' 'Tis but nature' was the general verdict. But . . . anything in the way of what they called 'loose living' was detested by them.

– Flora Thompson, Lark Rise *(1939)*

When the young Miles and Christopher Hutchinson turned into their rented beds at Cornsay in County Durham they did not at first know it, but they were only four miles south-west of where the teenaged Rosina Robson lived with her blind older sister Kate and their elderly parents at No. 27 Burnhope Colliery. When the connections were eventually made, the results would be explosive.

If Miles's first two decades had been turbulent and Rosina's relatively calm, the youngest daughter of the Robson family was about to overcompensate. Within three short years she would turn inside out her own life, Miles's life, the lives of their immediate families and neighbours and the lives of one or two accidental passers-by. Before she had reached the age of 20, Rosina Robson had taken her settled world in both strong hands and convulsed it so thoroughly that she and those in her immediate orbit had little choice but to set course for a new one.

Rosina had known a boy called George Hall since she was eight or nine years old. In the early 1870s, when Rosina was still a schoolgirl, her older sister Sarah had at the age of 21 met, courted, married and settled down to raise a family with a man from Billy Row named Thomas Hall.

Billy Row again. This was the same small industrial suburb of Crook-with-Billy-Row that was still in the early 1870s the home of the teenaged Miles Hutchinson and would remain the address of Miles's stepmother Louisa and his five half-brothers and sisters. Like Miles, like almost every other working male of the district, Thomas Hall was a coalminer and the son and the brother of coalminers.

'There were two Robson sisters married two Hall brothers,' their twentieth-century grandchildren would say. 'One of the Halls was a good man. The other was a waster.' The noun could have meant several things, none of them flattering. At bottom, it signified that its subject was a waste of time, a man who preferred idleness, or drink or violence or all three, to an ordinary, useful life.

The older brother, Thomas Hall, was not a waster. He made a home for Sarah and their daughter Elizabeth (who was named in typical tribute to Sarah's – and Rosina's – mother) at No. 185 Billy Row.

Next door, at No. 186 Billy Row, Sarah's (and Rosina's) older brother William Robson lived with his family – his wife, Harriet, who had come all the way from Cornwall in the far south-west of England, and their infant son and daughter. The conjunction of brother William's and sister Sarah's married homes was neither unusual nor coincidental. Members of the same family often lodged in neighbouring or adjacent pit cottages. It was an arrangement with which most colliery managers sympathised, and which they consequently facilitated.

For almost ten years, as she progressed from girlhood into her teens, Rosina Robson could travel nine miles from the parental home at Burnhope to visit both her sister Sarah and her brother William in the same street at Billy Row. In the course of that time she inevitably met and got to know her sister's husband's own Billy Row family. That family included a younger brother named George. George Hall was five years older than Rosina

Robson, but he would have been merely a 13-year-old school-boy when the little Robson girl first came to call.

They grew up, their age difference notwithstanding, in tandem; sharing during Rosina's visits to Billy Row the shadow of their older siblings' married lives. That they became close, a certain kind of close, is obvious. The depth and balance and character of their short, youthful relationship is and will remain obscure. Only one result of it would be as visible as visible can be.

Rosina Robson, this pretty, restless, assertive girl, made love with the 23-year-old George Hall, probably in the vicinity of Billy Row, certainly in the spring of 1882, a few months after her eighteenth birthday. 'Made love', that is, in the wholly physical twenty-first-century meaning, rather than the nineteenth-century expression of polite flirtation.*

George had by then been working in the local pit for almost ten years. He was unmarried and still lived with his mother and father. Rosina Robson returned the nine miles home to her parents' cottage in Burnhope, and woke up one morning in the summer of 1882 to the knowledge that she was pregnant.

She had been carrying their child for eight months before Rosina Robson and George Hall married in November 1882. The shotgun service was held at St Thomas's Church on a hillside overlooking Billy Row. None of George Hall's family attended the wedding. Rosina's mother, Elizabeth, served as her witness before vicar Joseph Roscamp. George's best man was an illiterate 52-year-old neighbour and workmate from Billy Row named John Stoker.

The newlyweds walked out of the vestibule of St Thomas's under a Norman archway. A country lane ran past the church. At the other side of the lane stood a low drystone wall broken by a stout wooden stile. The 19-year-old bride in her tight wedding dress may have been helped by her husband over that stile. From

* This was not so unusual as later generations might have imagined. A survey carried out in the 1950s by the 'psychiatrist and social reformer' Dr Eustace Chesser reported that almost one in five British women born in the last decades of the nineteenth century admitted to having engaged in premarital sex.

its topmost step Rosina could have gazed forever across the gentle folds of southern County Durham. It was a Saturday. The fields and woodland would have been shrouded at regular intervals by the steam, dust and smoke of working coal mines. If she did not pause to consider those familiar scenes, she may have glanced briefly down into the nearest houses of Billy Row. From the church, from the wall and the stile, Rosina could also see her married home.

She stepped onto a footpath which traversed a large meadow, downhill for a few hundred yards from the church and the stile to West Terrace in Billy Row, where Rosina and George would set up house in a two-up, two-down corner cottage.

The cohabitation of George and Rosina Hall in that end terrace in Billy Row lasted for no more than ten weeks. On Christmas Eve 1882, a month and a half after her wedding, Rosina gave birth in West Terrace to a baby boy. She christened him William, after her own father. At about the same time she finally decided that the other male in the house, the boy she had known since girlhood, the man who had become her lover, her husband and the father of her child, was a waster.

The meteorological office in Durham city, nine miles from Billy Row, recorded the December of 1882 and January of 1883 as being unusually wet, windy and cold. It was roughly twice as cold, twice as windy and a third again as wet as an average nineteenth-century Durham winter, and the average Durham winter is not warm. In the closing days of December 1882 or in the first weeks of January 1883, the 19-year-old mother pulled together her few belongings and clothes, took her infant son in her arms and walked away from George Hall and Billy Row.

She did not go very far, but she went forever. She walked north, up through the wide sloping meadow, over the stile and past St Thomas's Church. She walked through the winter's day across one of the highest and most exposed heaths in County Durham. For most of her journey she unwittingly followed the path which had been taken away from their own Billy Row home seven years earlier by Miles and Christopher Hutchinson.

But after two miles on the blasted open moor Rosina diverged from the Hutchinsons' route. She turned west and walked abruptly downhill into a sheltered and isolated valley named Hedley Hill, where another cluster of cottages surrounded yet another coal mine. She entered the warmth of No. 49 Hedley Hill. There she and baby William found temporary comfort and refuge with her older sister Mary, Mary's coalminer husband, James Allison, and their only child, Betsy.

That part of rural County Durham is a landscape of hollows and crests, with the human settlements mostly in the hollows and therefore mostly invisible to each other. Billy Row, from where Rosina had fled, was just four miles from Hedley Hill – and was as far out of sight as Madagascar. But there were exceptions to this rule. On almost every day of her time in Hedley Hill during 1883 Rosina Hall could look down the short, flat, cultivated floor of the dale and see clearly, just half an hour's slow walk away, another, larger mining settlement. She could see, she could almost touch, the terraces, shops and looming works of Cornsay Colliery, where the 26-year-old Miles Hutchinson was still employed, where he still lodged, and where he was still unmarried.

What are the chances that Miles had known Rosina's older brother and fellow coalminer William Robson a decade earlier in Billy Row? They are good. What are the chances that Miles had also known the Hall family into which Rosina had been obliged to marry? They are equally good. There were in the early 1870s perhaps 200 colliers in Billy Row. They mined the same few shafts and lived in the same cluster of terraces. Anybody who lived and worked as a coalminer in Billy Row for six years between 1869 and 1875, as Miles Hutchinson had done, was likely to know at least by sight most of his colleagues and neighbours.

What are the odds that Miles had seen, or even met, the young Rosina Robson when she visited her sister and brother in Billy Row while he was still living there in the early 1870s? They are impossible to quantify, but are less good. Miles was then a teenaged working coalminer; Rosina was almost half his age.

He was one miner among many; she was just another schoolgirl on holiday. Without a family connection, there was no obvious reason for either of them to take notice of the other.

In 1883 and 1884, in Hedley Hill and Cornsay, they quickly and enthusiastically made up for their earlier indifference. If they had met before, or noticed one another before, as young working man and schoolgirl, the preliminaries would have been easy. If not, there were plenty of reasons to notice each other now. Miles was 27 years old, more lean and handsome than ever, but fortuitously still unmarried. Rosina was, at the age of 19, already a woman with a past, but motherhood had turned her prettiness into something approaching beauty. She was strong in mind and body and her large dark eyes were invincibly set on a second and better future. To the rootless, wandering Miles Hutchinson, she was irresistible.

Exactly how irresistible is best demonstrated by what they did next.

Fairly quickly they agreed to marry. Before she could legally marry Miles Hutchinson, however, Rosina must divorce, or be divorced by, George Hall.

She could not do that. The reasons must have been Hall's rather than Rosina's. Throughout 1883 and into 1884 he did one of three things. He rejected outright her petition for divorce. Or he procrastinated and refused to discuss the matter. Or he temporarily disappeared.

The result was the same. By the beginning of 1884, a year after leaving him, Rosina was still legally bound to the absent father of her son, with no realistic possibility of untying the knot. This would have been profoundly annoying to any ordinary young woman. To Rosina Robson-Hall it was unbearable. She had a baby son in need of a real father, and a man with whom she had fallen in love was anxious to fill that vacancy. But unless George Hall agreed to a divorce, or until George Hall had been unjustifiably absent from her life for at least seven years, she could not legitimately marry Miles Hutchinson.

She decided to marry him anyway.

It was a dangerous step to take. Bigamy had been frowned upon by English criminal law for centuries. Until 1828, just 55 years earlier, convicted bigamists were liable to be hanged. The penalty had been moderated during the nineteenth century. Between 1828 and 1861 (when Miles Hutchinson was five years old) any person who 'being married, shall marry any other person during the life of the former husband or wife' was liable to transportation 'beyond the Seas for the Term of Seven years'. In short, had they attempted this felony two decades earlier, Rosina Robson-Hall-Hutchinson would have been looking at the possibility of a new life, or death, in a convict settlement on the fatal shore of Botany Bay in Australia.

In 1861 the Bigamy Act was repealed. Its replacement, which was still on the statute books in the early 1880s, substituted for transportation a maximum sentence of seven years' penal servitude and a minimum, mandatory sentence of three. The quid pro quo was straightforward. If Rosina and Miles Hutchinson were caught getting married in 1883 and 1884, she would have faced at least 36 months in Durham jail.

They were probably persuaded to go ahead and take the risk by another momentous family event at the end of 1883; an event which both motivated Miles and Rosina and offered them an escape from the possible consequences of her bigamy.*

In the last days of December 1883, a year after she had given birth to baby William and then walked away from George Hall, three

---

* George Hall does not come well out of this narrative, but it is worth considering that he might have been cheerfully complicit in Rosina's bigamy. George was probably as unwilling a husband to Rosina as she was a wife to him. But the divorce laws of the time made it almost impossible for one to achieve a legal separation from the other without vivid and undeniable evidence of physical abuse or of infidelity. In the case of such a separation, George Hall stood a good chance of being given custody of young William, and it is likely that he was as reluctant to be a father as he was to be a husband. So he could happily have struck a deal with Miles and Rosina. In exchange for his silence, he would be required to take no further responsibility for his first son and first wife. His complicity would not mollify a court of law, but it would reduce the prospect of Rosina's bigamy ever being aired before a magistrate.

of Rosina's older sisters emigrated to the United States of America. They sailed from Liverpool shortly after Christmas and arrived in the USA on 10th January 1884, to start a new life in a new country in the New Year.

Thirty-one-year-old Sarah, twenty-five-year-old Kate and twenty-two-year-old Rachel boarded the *British Crown* at Mersey docks in the company of two of their husbands and two of their children. Sarah travelled with her husband, Tom Hall, and daughter Elizabeth from Billy Row. Rachel, whose husband, James McCormack, was already waiting for them on the western side of the Atlantic Ocean, brought her three-year-old girl Eliza. And their blind and childless sister Kate took ship with her husband, Tom Wilkinson.

Rosina and Miles would surely have preferred to travel with them. But until her marital situation was somehow resolved, Rosina could not properly plan a new life. Miles in his turn may not have wished to run away with another man's wife and child. So for the moment they stayed behind, hoping and failing to wring a voluntary divorce out of George Hall.

In the early summer of 1884, seventeen months after Rosina had walked away from Hall and five months after her sisters had emigrated to the United States, they ran out of patience.

If they were to marry bigamously, they must do so in a place far enough from Cornsay and Hedley Hill and Billy Row that nobody – especially, perhaps, the vicar – would object to the reading of their wedding banns at services on three consecutive Sundays before the nuptial tie. They settled on St John's Church in the parish of Brandon. This establishment stood ten straight miles away from their homes. It was close enough for Rosina and Miles to travel there in a day, and close enough for another of Rosina's older married sisters, Elizabeth Watson, to attend the ceremony with her husband William and act as witnesses. And it was far enough away, this cluttered little township of Brandon, for the nervous couple to hope for anonymity, to assume with some confidence that neither the vicar nor any of his congregation would be aware that Miles Hutchinson's fiancee was already a married woman. As it turned out, that was a fair assumption.

Nonetheless, Rosina took care to disguise her identity. She described herself to Reverend Lawson of St John's Church, and in the banns which he duly announced, as a spinster whose name was Rosina Hall. That was half a lie. Rosina Hall she was; a spinster she was not. She then gave her father's name – for obvious reasons of consistency – as William Hall instead of William Robson. Her sister Elizabeth, her brother-in-law William and her bridegroom Miles all signed up to these deceits on the marriage certificate. When those three walked out of St John's Church, Brandon, on 14 June 1884 they were vulnerable to charges of aiding and abetting a felony. When Rosina walked out with them she was both a fraud and a bigamist. But she also walked out as Rosina Hutchinson, and she would cleave to that name up to and beyond the grave.

Elizabeth and William Watson, their fingers crossed, returned home to their working lives in the County Durham coalfield. Miles and Rosina Hutchinson picked up young William and the few possessions they could carry. Miles took his 19-year-old half-brother Christopher out of Cornsay Colliery and the group of four set off on foot for Liverpool.

They were all of them – Miles and Rosina and Christopher Hutchinson, Sarah and Tom Hall, Kate and Tom Wilkinson and Rachel McCormack – moved in those few months in 1884 by great coincidences. Their reasons for leaving Britain were as diverse and individual as the motives of every single one of the 23 million Europeans who emigrated to the United States of America between 1880 and 1930.

They were economic migrants, certainly. In the 1880s the British economy was depressed. In 1880 for the first time in history the per capita Gross Domestic Product of the United States was greater than that of the United Kingdom. British industry, even the essential coalmining industry, experienced lay-offs and disputes. 'The older industries,' writes the economic historian Peter Malthius, '. . . were not accepting innovations, or investing capital for re-equipment on a large enough scale.

Productivity was falling in coal mining faster in Britain than elsewhere . . . Rates of growth of industrial production had been above 3 per cent per annum since 1820; after 1880 they fell to below 2 per cent.' To add to the national woe the worst outbreak of Foot-and-Mouth disease on record spread havoc through the British livestock sector in the first years of the 1880s, raising the shop price of beef and mutton to unprecedented levels.★

But Miles and Rosina Hutchinson were also fleeing from a prison sentence for bigamy. Rosina had clearly been disowned or disinherited by her parents following her extra-marital pregnancy, her short-lived first marriage and her illegal second wedding. Miles, the restless, motherless young itinerant from Swaledale, had no parents left alive to disinherit him.

Miles and Christopher and the two Toms were also extracting themselves from serious industrial disputes in the Durham coalfield which would lead to a series of long and painful strikes. Although they knew, as did every coalminer in every coalfield in Britain, that the newly opened underground workings of Pennsylvania and Virginia were desperate for imported pitmen, they may have hoped to be able in the land of the free to cut themselves and their children loose from the hereditary occupation of mining. All four men, Tom Hall, Miles Hutchinson, Christopher Hutchinson and Tom Wilkinson, were the sons of miners and had worked in collieries since their early teens. But in passage to the USA they registered their occupations respectively as 'labourer', 'labourer', 'labourer' and optimistically, poignantly, in the case of Tom Wilkinson, 'farmer'. He was travelling to America. Why not dream?

A more fundamental vision provoked them all. They were going, in greater and lesser part, because sister Kate was blind.

★ Between 1880 and 1883 a total of 373,664 cattle and 355,628 sheep which were directly affected by Foot-and-Mouth were destroyed. This level of devastation would not be approached again until 2001, when in a prophylactic programme 594,000 cattle and 3,310,000 sheep were killed to prevent Foot-and-Mouth from spreading.

It was probably an item in a newspaper. Rosina was the only member of the party young enough to have been made fully literate by compulsory elementary schooling following the 1870 Education Act. We have already seen that Miles was among the 50 per cent of colliers of his generation who could not write a word; given his motherless childhood and adolescence it is likely that he was also among the minority who had difficulty in deciphering printed sentences. Rosina's sighted sisters were probably more literate. There was a reasonably high level of literacy and numeracy in their communities even before the arrival of state-sponsored education, due to evening classes, Methodist hedge schools and simple self-improvement. But levels of capability varied enormously and it is most likely that relevant pieces of news were read aloud by the likes of Rosina to Miles and Kate, and Rachel and Sarah and their husbands.

It was a small, shallow story at the foot of a slim column of type. It was headlined: 'AMERICAN DOCTOR CURES BLINDNESS. THE MAGNETICON MAKES PATIENTS SEE AGAIN. SEVERAL SUCCESSES CLAIMED'.

They would have tried with increasing frustration other feeble, old-fashioned British alleviatives for Kate's blindness. Porteous's Vegetable Ointment, for instance, had been advertised as both curing cancer and 'restoring vision'. But it would not have restored Kate's sight.

The Magneticon was vastly more plausible. From the very first line of print in Rosina's newspaper article, American magnetic therapy suggested actual scientific promise. Its waves of magnetic currents passing harmlessly through the body would rearrange a patient's isotopes and restore her damaged tissues and organs. This was no foul-smelling reduction of old shrubbery. This was mysteriously logical. Magnetic therapy was clean, modern, proven and attested. It was a new cure in a new age from the new world. It was transatlantic medical ingenuity. It was entirely credible and it provided the only acceptable reason for a blind woman, whose very sightlessness had caused her to be told and to accept that she would forever be incapable of bearing and raising children, to abandon the small familiar corners of her tied cottage, to leave behind the only sounds and sensations she had ever known and walk the width of England, sail across the Atlantic Ocean and lose herself in a measureless new continent.

So they would all go, for all of their manifold reasons and with all of their different hopes, to a land without beggars, rent, duty, overseers, kings, queens, bishops and gamekeepers. This gang of siblings, half-siblings, partners, in-laws and infants would go to a bounteous land where grazings were limitless and hay grew wild; where new mines were being sunk in rich young seams of lead and coal; where free men were willing to pay their equals fair money for a fair day's work.

Four men, four women and three children would go to a land where, somewhere, physicians or scientists could cure Kate's blindness. They would leave their dirty, troubled old world behind and walk to America.

Kate Wilkinson and Rosina Hutchinson were not alone in their faith in the restorative powers of electricity. In 1887 the American magazine *Electric Review* reported an interesting trend at the Capitol building in Washington DC. Congressmen were electrocuting themselves.

Down in the Capitol's engine room workmen had been urged to rig a connecting wire to the building's main electricity generator, and to hang a small brass chain from the railing around the generator's wheelbelt. Anybody who took hold of the wire and then completed a circuit by grasping the brass chain would enjoy a series of small electric shocks: a succession of pinpricks in the hands and arms.

The prevailing wisdom insisted that this was highly therapeutic. It was so beneficial that America's legislators, weary from 'receptions and suppers all night' or having 'exhausted their brainpower by speechmaking', or both, would retire to the Capitol's basement to be 'filled quietly with electricity'. Having been infused, quickly, efficiently and free of charge, with a dose of electrical energy, reinvigorated congressmen could return – taking the basement stairs two at a time – to the podium and the dinner table.

The Hutchinsons' task – which promised to be an easy one in the United States of America – was to find an electro-therapist who specialised in curing not only fatigue, hangovers, rheumatism and cancer, but also blindness.

Rosina, Miles, Christopher and William Hutchinson walked to the Atlantic port of Liverpool from County Durham in the early December of 1884. They walked because they were the last generation in the developed world for whom walking was the default method of transport. In that modest respect they represented the final few links in a chain which reached back two million years to the ramble out of Africa of Homo Erectus. Their nineteenth-century civilisation provided other forms of locomotion. The Hutchinsons were familiar with horses, carriages and railway trains. But they were poor and provident people; walking was free, and they were comfortable on foot. Groups of working men, women and children could, and if necessary did, tramp distances of 40 or 50 miles a day, even when burdened with packs or infants. Walking to Liverpool was neither a challenge nor an imposition. It was simply the obvious thing to do.

The 150-mile hike took them, in the short winter daylight hours, almost a week. Their obvious route was a poignant one, reversing Miles' and Christopher's steps 15 years earlier out of the Yorkshire Dales. At the end of the first day they will have found themselves clear of the Durham coalfield and entering the wide green pastures at the mouth of Swaledale. They walked through Reeth, where Miles's birth and later the death of his mother had been registered almost 30 years earlier. They walked beside the River Swale, between the icy hedgerows of Cloggerby Rigg and into and out of his birthplace at Thwaite. They slept on warm hay in barns, they ate bread and cheese, they were offered milk and tea by residents on their route. They washed in and drank from the fast, cold becks.

They cleared the Swale's watershed by the few bleak frost-bitten walls of Gothgill and for the first time in any of their lives they saw the Irish Sea. They walked down towards Lancaster and the tidal plain of Morecambe Bay. They walked due south along the flat, farmed eastern seaboard. There were smoking mill valleys and the high, snow-capped Pennines to their left and there was boundless salt water to their right. They walked into the city of Liverpool.

It was a taste of towns to come. They had never seen anything like it. The port on the Mersey had over 600,000 inhabitants – which was four times that of Newcastle and almost twice as many people as the entire population of the county of Durham – and it was growing by the day. Liverpool's founding engagements in the cotton and slave trades had been supplemented and slowly replaced by its role as the principal English point of departure and arrival to and from the United States of America, and by hundreds of thousands of Irish immigrants. When Miles, Rosina, Christopher and William Hutchinson arrived there at the end of 1884 more than one quarter of the population of Liverpool was Irish.★

It was a port like all such industrial ports, but on an imperial scale. It made its money sharply and unsentimentally from goods and humans in transit. Its people's caustic dialect, their unique, persistent blend of western Lancashire and rural Ireland, would have been conversant with the drawl of the north-east of England only if Liverpudlians clipped their tongues and if both parties modified their vowels. With those compromises made, the Hutchinson family would have had no difficulty in being directed to Waterloo Dock, introduced to

★ In the following year, 1885, Liverpool would become the first and last place in England, Scotland or Wales to elect an Irish Nationalist Member of Parliament to the House of Commons in London. T.P. O'Connor from Athlone in County Westmeath would represent at Westminster his country-men and constituents in the Liverpool Scotland ward (so-called because it was located around the Irish quarter of Scotland Road) for fully 44 years, between 1885 and his death in 1929.

an American Line shipping agent, buying £2.00 steerage tickets to the United States aboard the SS *British Crown*, finding a nearby flophouse and waiting for their vessel to lower the gangplanks.

They sailed from Liverpool on 11th December 1884. As well as the Hutchinsons the *British Crown* carried 139 other passengers, almost all of them English and Irish working-class families.

Aside from such phenomena as the Pilgrim Fathers, and despite having planted their language, legal system and games in half of the earth, the English (as opposed to the Irish, or even the Scots) are not usually considered to have been one of the great emigrant races. But they were.

Between 1881 and 1890 almost two million British – which was then to say English, Scottish, Welsh and Irish – citizens emigrated to the United States of America. They represented almost 30 per cent of all new arrivals in the USA at that time. The Irish, from their small native population, constituted a disproportionately large fraction of American immigrants from Great Britain.

But in blunt numerical quantities, as many English and Welsh citizens as Irish men and women travelled to the USA. In the quarter-century between 1871 and 1895, 1,334,000 English and Welsh people crossed the Atlantic to the USA – which was exactly the same number as travelled from Ireland. Between them, the English, Irish and Welsh accounted for 26 per cent of all American immigrants. (The Scottish presence was smaller, totalling less than 3 per cent of American immigrants.)

This small family group from the Tyne and Wear coalfield was therefore part of a huge English historical phenomenon. They were a tiny sample of the million English and Welsh working people who fled their country for the USA in the single decade of the 1880s. They were an even tinier microcosm of the six million ordinary Britons who arrived in the United States – having abandoned home and hope in London, Glamorgan, Cork, Connemara, Inverness-shire and County Durham – between 1853 and 1905.

As individuals they signified little. As part of a monumental movement they represented a great deal. The population of the whole of Great Britain in 1881 was 35,000,000 – which was roughly the average population of the growing nation in the second half of the nineteenth century. The six million English, Irish, Scottish and Welsh citizens who went from Britain to the United States alone (another three million went to Australia, Canada and elsewhere) in those last 50 years of Queen Victoria's reign were equivalent to one fifth of the average total population of Britain in their time.

They were not all the starving Irish or dispossessed Highland Scots, as a later popular mythology would insist. Fully half of them were English. In each calendar year of the single decade between 1881 and 1890, one out of every 400 English citizens left his or her native country for the United States. Not to the other white colonies or far-flung countries favoured by British rule – although Australia, Canada and the Indian sub-continent did as we have seen receive hundreds of thousands of English escapees – but to the free former colony which was the USA. By the time the 1880s were done, English emigrants to the United States alone had totalled in those ten years almost a million people. They were the Hutchinsons, Halls and Wilkinsons: the forgotten English emigrants, the millions of deserters from the heartland of the largest economy, greatest military and political power and most expansive empire in the world.

Two weeks after weighing anchor at Liverpool's Waterloo Dock, on young William's second birthday, the *British Crown* cruised slowly up the lower 100 miles of the Delaware River. Her 143 emigrants looked out over the Delaware bay and the broad river mouth to the hazy eastern fringes of that landmass which, as 40 years later an American author would write of them and their fellows, was at last commensurate with their capacity for wonder.

After ten hours' steaming up the Delaware, Rosina Hutchinson had finally gazed upon the other Philadelphia, the namesake and inspiration of the tiny coalmining settlement in County Durham where her mother had been born 63 years earlier. She saw a massive city, a metropolis larger even than Liverpool – but one whose unimaginable hinterland, sprawling boundlessly towards the empty horizon on either side of the Delaware roads, dwarfed it like a country hamlet.

The 21st-century Amtrak carriage rolls along a nineteenth-century track between Philadelphia and Pittsburgh. I sat in it and thought of Victorian emigrants.

There is a way of viewing, a way of looking at things, which ought to be called Historian's Eye. It involves gazing at a landscape, or a townscape, or even in some parts of the world a busy seascape, and mentally removing from view everything that was not there in, say, 1885. With a bit of practice even an amateur may then develop an internally generated image of a lost world. In certain places Historian's Eye is a relatively easy exercise – old Marrakech springs to mind, once you've divorced the citizenry from its mopeds and mobile phones. In others it is not worth attempting: Manhattan would be virtually razed to the ground.

As a rule of thumb, Historian's Eye is easier in the countryside than the towns. It is easier in unpopulated rural parts than in farming areas (the emptier the better – Historian's Eye is probably redundant in the Sahara Desert). And it is easy enough even in central Pennsylvania . . . bleach out that highway and that silo, substitute a smaller dwelling for that substantial farmhouse, factor in a few more trees here and there and – it's the nineteenth century!

I was playing that game with great satisfaction during a rest-stop at a lonely Mifflin County railway station when out of my nineteenth-century mindscape there appeared a nineteenth-century family group in a nineteenth-century horse-drawn carriage.

Seven or eight men, women and children dismounted, approached and boarded the train. They were dressed plainly and comfortably; the women uniformly in long, full skirts, navy blue or white capes and aprons and the bearded, long-haired men in dark coats and black felt hats. The adults spoke quietly to one another. A boy barked a question in a guttural dialect and was quietened by a warning glance.

I caught the conductor's eye. 'Amish?' I asked. 'Yes,' he said. And then, nicely protective of his compatriots from the condescension of a European: 'Just ordinary folk.'

They were once known as Pennsylvania Dutch. They were not from the Netherlands and they did not speak Dutch. They were members of a sect of Lutherans named Old Order Anabaptists. The defining characteristic of Anabaptism is probably the one which is reflected in its name. Anabaptists consider that only true believers can feasibly be baptised. This rules out the baptism of infants, and in such strict Anabaptist communities as the Amish, only fully fledged adults may be received unto Christ. Such a practice, or non-practice, as the failure to baptise the newly born was and is regarded as heretical by the Roman Catholic Church.

Many such fledgling Protestant sects existed in post-Reformation Europe. This one owed its foundation to the convictions of a Swiss divine named Jakob Ammann, and they therefore called themselves Amish. Following decades of persecution by the established Roman Catholic Church and its affiliated nation states, and profound, discomforting disagreements with other Protestant orders, the Amish began in the eighteenth century to emigrate from their homelands in Switzerland and Alsace. Their chosen refuge was the commonwealth of religious tolerance which had been established by the English Quaker William Penn on the east coast of North America. Within little over 100 years there were perhaps 5,000 Amish in Pennsylvania and none at all left in Europe. And there in Pennsylvania they quietly multiplied for a further half-century until the rest of the United States began to discover them. They were the idealisation of one-way emigrants. Their life of the guiding spirit made the location of their earthly home irrelevant. They were known to their American neighbours as the Plain People. They called their neighbours Englishers.

They were not universally tolerated. The Connecticut pastor Leonard Woolsey Bacon wrote in 1897 of:

Group after group of picturesque devotees that had been driven into seclusion and eccentricity by long and cruel persecution – the Tunkers, the

Schwenkfelders, the Amish – kept coming [to America] and bringing with them their traditions, their customs, their sacred books, their timid and pathetic disposition to hide by themselves, sometimes in quasi-monastic communities . . . sometimes in actual hermitage, as in the ravines of the Wissahickon . . . This migration of the German sects [to be distinguished from the later migration from the established Lutheran and Reformed churches] furnished the material for that curious 'Pennsylvania Dutch' population which for more than two centuries has lain encysted, so to speak, in the body politic and ecclesiastic of Pennsylvania, speaking a barbarous jargon of its own, and refusing to assimilate with the surrounding people.

In 1920 Yale University Press's Chronicles of America textbooks would dismiss

. . . the Amish, Old and New, whose ridiculous singularity of dress, in which they discarded all ornaments and even buttons, earned them the nickname 'Hooks and Eyes'. But no matter how aloof these sects held themselves from the world, or what asceticism they practiced upon themselves, or what spiritual and economic fraternity they displayed to each other, they possessed a remarkable native cunning in bargaining over a bushel of wheat or a shoat, and for a time most of their communities prospered.

They were not always and everywhere subjected to the scorn of rival churchmen or the snobbery of academics. When in 1895 an elderly Amish man named William Hertel had his house burned down and seven-acre potato crop uprooted by 'a gang of thirty hoodlums' in Ohio, it was reported that Hertel was 'the object of the grossest outrage . . . another victim of superstition', and that 'the better class of [non-Amish] citizens is organising a movement to put a stop to the outrages'.

In 1888 the New York Times discovered the Pennsylvania Amish to be 'a plain, unpretentious sect of farmers who wear broad-brimmed hats and hooks and eyes on their clothes instead of buttons'. The abandonment of this traditional garb by a young man named Amos Kurtz, said the Times, had led to Kurtz's excommunication – an event which the young rebel promptly celebrated 'by a party, at which there was an abundance of refreshments, and the village band furnished music'.

The uniquely powerful roots which the Amish had carried from Alsace and Switzerland – roots which they would sink deeper into the fertile soil of North America than those of any other race or creed – were not immediately apparent. As the nineteenth century turned into the twentieth, terms like 'barbarous' (which was about as inapplicable to the pacifist Amish as it was possible to be) and 'native cunning' (which aimed enviously at the Amish's extraordinary farming skills) fell slowly into disrepute. Unaware of and unmoved by the replacement of such descriptions by words like 'quaint', the Amish continued to grow in numbers while largely rejecting as corrupting of their simple creed such perfectly American conveniences as power-line electricity, automobiles, clothing buttons and insurance policies.

When you get your eye in, you see Amish all over the twenty-first-century northern states. They stand out somehow, in their a-stylish uniforms, like extras in their own period drama. They present a real problem to Historian's Eye, when you see them walking down a Pittsburgh street. You can neither delete nor properly include them. They represent no era but their own. They were white American immigrants like no other. They came, they stayed and they prospered as both the antithesis of the body politic of the United States and the living embodiment of the American Dream.

5

Hell with the Lid Taken Off

Pittsburgh, Pennsylvania, 1885

Pittsburgh is . . . without exception the blackest place which I ever saw . . . Nothing can be more picturesque than the site . . . Even the filth and wondrous blackness of the place are picturesque when looked down upon from above. The tops of the churches are visible, and some of the larger buildings may be partially traced through the thick, brown, settled smoke. But the city itself is buried in a dense cloud.

— *Anthony Trollope,* North America *(1860)*

They journeyed by train, westward beyond the Schuylkill River. They left the industrial buildings and tenements quickly behind, and as the haze of Philadelphia's smokestacks faded in the east they passed through a boundless sweep of naked countryside. Their train rattled past mile after mile after mile of snow-covered meadow and woodland. Reclaimed pastureland rolled towards an apparently boundless and infinitely renewable horizon, but in this huge and empty landscape there was little sign of its reclaimers, or even of their stock.

The English family will have sat on facing wooden benches on the train. We can sketch an impression: Blind Kate, wrapped tightly in a coat and a woollen shawl against the cold, knitting quickly and confidently. Miles Hutchinson and Tom Wilkinson stretching out their legs from the window seats, and alternating wary glances at their luggage on the floor beneath their seats and at the continent outside. Rosina's two-year-old son sleeping in her lap. All the windows were closed. The carriage smelled of meat and sweat and unwashed clothes and warm breath and burning tobacco. A spittoon sloshed gently by the wall. Men dozed and smoked pipes in the overhead sleeping racks. Women served food from iron pots. Children ran up and down the wide central aisle. A cat drank milk from a bowl on the bare floor and a dog was tied to a supporting pillar. Uniformed guards and conductors ambled confidently by.

The stopping train between Philadelphia and Pittsburgh would take a little more – nobody, not even the Pennsy guys, the employees of the Pennsylvania Railroad Company, was perfectly sure how much more – than eight hours to cover 300 miles.

It passed through scattered hamlets with both foreign and familiar names – Downingtown, Paoli, Ardmore. But mostly it passed through a landscape that to European eyes was unimaginably deserted. Hours and scores of miles went by without the hint of a house or a person or a domesticated animal. They wound slowly up high mountains, through quiet forests, beside fantastic lakes and rivers, across the eastern continental divide and down into the open heartlands of America. And there it felt vaguely as though they had passed through another gate, crossed another ocean, left yet another world behind, taken themselves into another unknown.

Beyond that watershed the rolling pastureland and the lonely little settlements resumed. At such halts as Lewistown they would look out at wooden fences and a large barn, at a solitary plume of smoke rising from a single house two miles away, or five, or ten, or more . . . the continent dizzily defied their sense of perspective.

They are likely to have encountered Amish, but they may not even have noticed. It is likely that transient Englishers who crossed paths with Amish saw little to remark upon. Like the Irish in County Durham, they were merely other immigrants in a sea of immigrants. In 1885 it was only their rejection of buttons and moustaches which superficially distinguished the Amish from anybody else on a train between Philadelphia and Pittsburgh. And the Amish *Ordnung* had always tolerated trains.

It would probably have been late in the evening when their scheduled stopping train rolled into the industrial ferment of Pittsburgh. The Hutchinsons and Wilkinsons, veterans of the Tyne and Wear coalfield, had arrived in what was arguably the filthiest metropolis on earth. By day this city was 'the blackest, dirtiest, grimiest place in the United States . . .' 'smoke, smoke, smoke – everywhere smoke . . .'. By night, according to the English-born writer James Parton, it was 'Hell with the lid taken off.'

Pittsburgh had been founded on a promontory where the Allegheny and Monongahela rivers converged in a giant letter Y into the single enormous stream of the Ohio river. This promontory, the central tine in the river-fork, and the banks of both rivers on either side of the Y were by 1885 bulging with scores of steel mills, glass works and other heavy industries. In the daylight hours their smokestacks blanketed Pittsburgh in soot and smog. At night the ochre and orange flames from their blast furnaces lit up the gloomy sky. Twenty years earlier in 1862, another Englishman, the novelist Anthony Trollope, a man who was familiar with the dark Satanic mills of the British industrial revolution, had declared Pittsburgh to be 'without exception, the blackest place I ever saw . . . The city itself is buried in a dense cloud'.

Both authors, Parton and Trollope, were writing of Pittsburgh in the 1860s, when the city was an unpolluted Arcadia compared with what it would become within twenty years. In 1860 Pittsburgh's population was 50,000; by 1880 it had grown to 156,000. Its boom was built on iron and steel, which in turn were built on coal.

In 1865, at the end of the American Civil War which had greatly increased demand for the city's produce, Pittsburgh's furnaces turned out two fifths of all the iron in the USA. But in the decade after the war the price of iron fell sharply and Pittsburgh's mainstay industry appeared to be in decline. Then in 1872 a 37-year-old immigrant from Scotland who had prospered as a bond salesman and by investing acutely in

American railroads, bridges and oil derricks, made a journey home to Britain.

There Andrew Carnegie visited at his manufactory in Sheffield a British ironmaster named Henry Bessemer. Bessemer's pioneering method of converting molten iron to steel convinced Carnegie that the industrial iron age was over and the day of steel was about to dawn. He was right. Just as Bessemer's choice of Sheffield in England for the site of his steel mill would determine that city's manufacturing destiny for the following century, Carnegie would go back across the Atlantic, announce to his partners 'The day of iron is past! Steel is king!' and do exactly the same for Pittsburgh. Andrew Carnegie, with the whole of the booming United States as his market, would become immeasurably the wealthier man.

Like the old iron furnaces, steel mills were fired by coal. Pennsylvania was rich in coal. Seams had been commercially mined in the Commonwealth since the 1830s, when Philadelphian investors first sank their money into the exploitation of anthracite, a hard and pure coal which is difficult to fire but which, once alight, burns with a fierce and steady heat. The investors got their money back. Ninety-five per cent of all the anthracite coal in the USA turned out to lie beneath the soil of the rural counties north and west of Philadelphia.

The iron and steel town of Pittsburgh was 300 miles west of the Philadelphian anthracite mines, and it stood smack in the middle of one of the biggest bituminous coalfields in the western world. The Pittsburgh Basin bituminous coal deposits covered 15,000 square miles east, west, north and south of the city itself, and had been exploited as far back as the 1760s. Bituminous coal is neither so pure nor so hot as anthracite coal. Anthracite coal is virtually smokeless, while burning bituminous coal produces intense black clouds of hydrocarbon gases and fumes.

Bituminous coal is, however, most suitable for coking. Coking coal was then essential for iron and steel production. And back in the north-east of England the Hutchinsons, Halls and Wilkinsons had gained all of their colliery experience in mining for the local equivalent of deep-seam bituminous coal. So it was that in western Pennsylvania in the middle of the 1880s their interests coincided briefly with those of Andrew Carnegie.

They will have alighted in 1885 on a makeshift platform on the south bank of the Monongahela river. It was a temporary platform because eight years earlier the old established railway station had been burned to the ground, after the Pennsylvania Railroad Company reduced its employees' wages by 10 per cent and simultaneously cut back on staff by cutting the crews on freight trains. America was in economic depression at the time, and the action resulted in one of the first great American summer city riots. Imported troops fired upon a protesting assembly in the railway yards. Some 20 people were killed and many others injured. The surviving 'mob' returned that Saturday night, seized guns and ammunition from city-centre shops and drove the garrison out of its billet at a railway roundhouse.

There followed throughout the Sunday of 22 July an extraordinary – and by British standards, quite unfamiliar – carnival of destruction. One thousand six hundred railway carriages and a hundred and twenty-six locomotives were destroyed. Much of the city centre, including the railway station, was burned out. It was a 24-hour weekend insurrection: by Monday morning the flames were dying; on Tuesday the governor of Pennsylvania arrived with state and federal troops; by Wednesday the press could nervously report that although the railway workers continued to strike 'this city continues to be in a quiet condition'. Basic freight railway traffic would not be resumed until the following week, on Monday, 30 July, by which time Pittsburgh was beginning to run out of food and public sympathy for the strikers was ebbing. Shortly afterwards the railwaymen returned to work on the conditions of their employers. Their legacy was not to be restored jobs and pay-levels, but the physical evidence which lingered for years of the New World's raw and combustible industrial relations. In 1885 our small family group from

County Durham stepped into some of that vestigial evidence. It would have impressed them. They were hard and resilient people. They were accustomed to bosses' laws and the friction caused by their enforcement. But during even the worst disputes back home in England, nobody had yet carbonised Durham Railway Station.

They were probably met at Pittsburgh's makeshift railway platform. With or without Rosina's brother-in-law Thomas Hall, or any other acclimatised member of their advance guard, they walked on to lodgings outside the commercial district. They left behind paved streets and tramlines and walked onto dirt roads puddled with slush and banked by sooty snow. There were animal and human faeces underfoot. They smelled ammonia from the roaring riverside blast furnaces. The Hutchinsons and Wilkinsons can be conjured only like spirits in the rowdy tenement streets of downtown Pittsburgh: the men with large bags slung easily across their backs; Rosina with the sleeping William's small head on her shoulder; Kate with her hand resting lightly on her husband's arm.

Peter Krass, a biographer of Andrew Carnegie who was also the great-grandson of a nineteenth-century Pittsburgh mill-worker would, writing 80 years later, describe those streets as . . .

putrefied . . . There were few water lines available to flush the stinking excrement and garbage, because in a bout of perfect logic, the Pittsburgh City Council's Water Commission had decided that the size of a water pipe being laid on a given street would be determined by the amount of potential revenue it would bring; in other words, big pipes were laid in the rich neighbourhoods, while the poor tenement districts in desperate need of water were granted smaller pipes that fed communal outlets . . .

The Pittsburgh Board of Health declared the tenement homes 'the filthiest and most disagreeable locality within the limits of the city', where people were renting 'the merest apologies for houses', the structures characterised as 'tumble down houses in rows'. Most were dilapidated brick or frame buildings that provided no ventilation in the hot summers and were cold and damp in the winters. The neighbourhoods around the mills were populated with churches, taverns and brothels . . . Thousands of men fell to typhoid over the years, when, to quench their thirst after a hot day in the mills, they drank directly from Pittsburgh's polluted Monongahela and Allegheny rivers.

People of all ages died here frequently and easily. The very young were often lucky to survive.

They will finally have stopped outside a tenement flophouse and bar filled with working men who had chosen whisky and beer over the poisonous water of the Monongahela.

Whiskey was considered medicinal by the workers looking to clear the dust from their throats and to soothe their aching muscles and bruised bones . . . ambivalent men in patched cotton trousers and sweat-stained shirts open at the collar. Dark lines of soot marked the creases in the skin around their mouth and eyes . . . All the men in the mill had reason to be ornery characters . . . There was no time for rest and relaxation. They worked seven-day weeks, and the only holidays granted by the mill-owners were Christmas and the Fourth of July.

Anthony Trollope had earlier stayed, not in such a hovel but in one of Pittsburgh's better hotels. The novelist wrote of his room there that it was 'not black to the eye, for the eye teaches itself to discriminate colours even when loaded with dirt, but black to the touch. On coming out of a tub of water my foot took an impression from the carpet exactly as it would have done had I trod bare-footed on a path laid with soot. I thought that I was turning negro upwards, till I put my wet hand upon the carpet, and found that the result was the same.'

And in the morning the family moved on to their new home in the coal patch.

The coal which fired the mills and furnaces of Pittsburgh was mostly mined outside town. The British soldiers who had in the eighteenth century manned the original Fort Pitt on the promontory between two rivers, cut coal out of the ground to keep themselves warm. This tradition of families digging their own domestic fuel was still alive in the town and its surrounds at the end of the nineteenth century and would continue well into the twentieth century.

Unhindered in North America by the hereditary mineral rights enforced by estate owners back in Europe, miners and others often opened their own miniature collieries in the back lot, or in the rough hillsides around their homes. In 1871 an artist named Harry Fenn (who was born in Richmond, England, in 1845 but emigrated to the United States and settled in New Jersey in 1865) came across just such a 'family coal mine' in the Pittsburgh area and made an engraving of it for *Every Saturday* magazine. Fenn showed the entrance to a small timber-propped mine shaft. A grimy young girl carrying a coal scuttle and a lit candle stood in its entrance. Nearby her brother rested on the ground, his short pick stabbed into the earth beside him. Between them a pair of makeshift wooden rails – like a ladder without rungs – ran up a steep hillside to their house. A soapbox full of the household coal that he had just cut and she had just carried was being hauled on four rickety wheels up the wooden rails by their father cranking a windlass at the top of the rise. Next to father and to the house stood a large pile of cut, carried, hauled and stored domestic coal.

Pittsburgh was, like the north-east of England, built on coal. But commercial mining required capital investment and bigger returns than could be transported in a soap box. The large deep shafts which fired the city's industries (as opposed to some of its domestic hearths) were therefore mostly sunk from necessity in the wide open spaces of Pittsburgh's rural hinterland. On such 'coal patches', as in the colliery villages of Great Britain, miners' houses and company stores were raised. 'A coal patch,' wrote one former western Pennsylvanian resident about her childhood, 'is a town where everything is built and owned by the coal company, including schools, churches, theaters, and residential structures . . .

> It is common for the mining camp and services to be built near the portal or entrance of the mine. A company town is designed for efficient housing. It . . . has identical housing units, and includes services built and operated by the company, such as a company store, an infirmary, and some recreational facilities. The company may also provide such services as free fuel, a church, schools and athletic facilities. Unlike many other industries mining does not typically come into an already established community. The mine entrance and availability of transport come first; housing for the workers usually follows. This arrangement made the company not only the miner's employer, but his landlord and storekeeper as well.

Throughout the 1870s and 1880s miners flocked from all over Europe to such Pennsylvanian coal patches. To many if not most of them the new life represented an improvement in both present conditions and in prospects over their old life in Silesia or the Pannonian Basin. But to immigrants from the north-east of England, to men and women attracted at least in part by the American dream of a country without rent, duty or overseers, it represented a reluctant step back towards the Tommy Shop and corporate control. They would nonetheless stay in the coal patch for varying but reasonable periods of time for four main reasons. The reasons were, in no particular order: because they found paid work; because the money thus earned was necessary if they were – as some of them certainly were – contemplating moving anywhere else; because those earnings could also help to finance Kate Wilkinson's blindness cure; and because Miles and Rosina Hutchinson, who would have a busy and productive sex life throughout their marriage, were expecting the birth of a child.

As native English-speakers the Hutchinsons, Halls, Wilkinsons and McCormacks were in a minority on their patch. They were probably in a small minority. Two decades later, a generation after the first great wave of Europeans washed into the Pennsylvanian coalfields, the Dillingham Immigration Commission would report to the United States Congress that it was still the case that no fewer than 76 per cent of the men who worked in the coal mines around Pittsburgh had been born outside the USA.★ 'The term "American miner",' said Senator William Dillingham of Vermont, 'so far as the western Pennsylvania field is concerned, is largely a misnomer.'

Belonging to that minority was to an Englishman's professional advantage. Their ability to speak fluently the same language as their new employers, coupled with their previous mining experience and their status as First World Europeans, found the men – who had in England all been coal-face hewers – more elevated and better-paid positions. Christopher Hutchinson, Thomas Hall and James McCormack walked into work as sinkers, which is to say that they directed the digging and opening of new shafts. It was not an easy number and it was not without peril. A sinker was obliged to go down with his shaft, to follow personally at close quarters its excursion into the ground, to correct its line and route through soil and shale and rock and into the widest seam of coal. Sinkers were injured and sinkers were killed. But if it was not quite the rolling fertile farm of Tom Wilkinson's fantasy, it still beat working at the coal face.

And yet, and yet . . . American industry might have been booming; Pittsburgh industry booming more than most; bituminous coal might have been in steadily increasing demand, but there was still no guaranteed weekly, monthly or yearly employ-

---

★ The Dillingham Commission, which expressed a highly influential racial distaste for eastern and southern Europeans, took pains to exclude certain other transatlantic nationalities from its inferred abhorrence. Slavs and Sicilians were fair game; white Anglo-Saxon Protestants were not. Dillinger carefully spelled out that less than 8 per cent of that 76 per cent of foreign colliers came originally from the developed, friendly, acceptable settler nations of Britain and Germany. If all of them had done so, the Commission implied, if all 76 per cent were British or German rather than Polish or Ukrainian, nobody could reasonably object.

ment in the Pennsylvania collieries. They sent coal upon demand to Andrew Carnegie and their other customers. When no immediate demand existed the coalmines did not open, the miners did not work and nobody was paid. Only on the evening of any given day would the coalowner signal, through two or three blasts on the colliery's steam whistle, that he would be open and hiring the following morning. One single doleful blast meant that he would not. The single blast was heard too frequently for comfort. The average wage was around $14.00 a week, but most miners were paid for fewer than half the number of days in a year. Less than 10 per cent – the 10 per cent of most valuable workers, a category which would usually but not always have included sinkers – could expect to work for ten months in the year. There was uncertainty here, insecurity of a kind which was only too familiar to men and women raised in the nineteenth-century Tyne and Wear field.

There was also an unfamiliar menace and brutality in the non-unionised American pits. Those jerry-built suburbs were garrisoned, defended and held to order by a company of men unknown in Britain, if not in some other parts of Europe, and regarded with fear and suspicion by immigrant miners. The Coal and Iron Police were revealingly known by eastern European workers as the 'Cossacks', and by others as the 'Yellow Dogs'. They were a private force ill-advisedly sanctioned in 1866 by the Pennsylvania Assembly. They would become the most notoriously unscrupulous of company police forces. Effectively unregulated, a law only unto themselves and their bosses, they were employed and paid by the various coal companies, which in turn donated to the State of Pennsylvania a dollar for every Yellow Dog hired (by the time of their dissolution in 1931 following one brutal judicial murder too many of a working man, almost 8,000 Coal and Iron Policemen had been commissioned). Their function was supposedly to protect company property. In practice they became an armed and mounted gang of vigilantes, an oppressive, violent, strike-breaking posse of 'common gunmen, hoodlums and adventurers'. They were known to be capable of kidnap, rape and casual killing. Even to those families such as the Hutchinsons which did not attract their hostility, the Coal and Iron Police were a constantly disturbing presence in the patches; a daily discomforting reminder of the vulnerability of immigrant working life in the American coal-fields.

In 1881 and 1885 the Pennsylvania Legislature had passed a number of laws regulating for greater safety and first-aid provision in its mines. But foremen and shift bosses were renowned for beating the weaker and more susceptible of their workers into greater efforts. 'Yes sir, I got clubbed often,' testified one man later with a phlegmatism which indicated that his was not an isolated experience. 'He would come around and club you and call you a son-of-a-bitch and [say] "quicker, quicker" . . .' Experienced miners, particularly experienced western European miners such as Miles and Christopher and the two Toms, were unlikely to bow to such treatment. They were more likely to be among the recalcitrant groups which refused to be awed by the 'foreman's authority . . . They stopped working and usually sat down when he entered their [working area]. If the foreman gave instructions, he presented them as suggestions.'

In and out of the deep pit shafts, like industrial working-class communities anywhere else, they developed their own insular, defensive strategies and culture into which no outsider – even an outsider with supposedly higher authority – could easily intrude. The evolution of this culture in the Pennsylvanian coalfields was undoubtedly hindered by its unique, unprecedented blend of different and mutually incomprehensible languages, religions, superstitions and habits. But if the coal patch workforce and community were to survive they had to adapt and learn to live and labour together. They did so with remarkable speed.

A small, rosy-cheeked white-haired Irishwoman who moved and worked in these communities at that time left both her memories and her nickname behind in the folklore of the coal patches. Mary Harris Jones was probably in her 40s in the 1880s (her exact date of birth in County Cork is uncertain). Having been a schoolteacher in Toronto and Tennessee she was appalled by what she saw in the industrial states. 'Before 1899 the coalfields of Pennsylvania were not organized,' Mother Jones would record:

> Immigrants poured into the country and they worked cheap. There was always a surplus of immigrant labor, solicited in Europe by the coal companies, so as to keep wages down to barest living. Hours of work down under ground were cruelly long. Fourteen hours a day was not uncommon, thirteen, twelve.
>
> The life or limb of the miner was unprotected by any laws. Families lived in company-owned shacks that were not fit for their pigs. Children died by the hundreds due to the ignorance and poverty of their parents. Often I have helped lay out for burial the babies of the miners, and the mothers could scarce conceal their relief at the little ones' deaths. Another was already on its way, destined, if a boy, for the breakers; if a girl, for the silk mills where the other brothers and sisters already worked.

They settled in this surprisingly unpromising place among Poles and Austro-Hungarians, Russians and people from the Baltic states. As the Dillingham Commission would later point out, immigration to the United States from eastern Europe in this period far exceeded immigration from any and all of the British Isles. The average $14.00 a week pay packet earned in the Pennsylvania mines was twice as much as a man could expect to take home in sterling from a British coalfield. But it was twenty or thirty times more than the dismal weekly income of a Scandinavian, Polish or even an Austrian peasant or hired hand in the 1880s. Many continental European men – Poles and Italians prominent among them – had been raised in a culture where seasonal emigration to earn hard cash abroad, at the bountiful harvests of rural France or the manufactories of urban Germany, was a routine of the calendar year. The arrival of fast, cheap steamship routes from European ports to the United States enabled them to cross the Atlantic to raise dollars rather than walk to Bordeaux and earn francs. Tens of thousands of them consequently did so each year. Many if not most of those Slavs and Latins had no real intention of staying forever in North America. Thousands saved just enough to buy extra stock and another acre of land at home, or build a new house, or afford to take a wife. Even those whose exile in the United States lasted for decades rather than months or years often returned to Slovenia, Galicia or the Mezzogiorno at the end of their working lives, to see out their days as replanted 'Americanos' or 'Amerikanski' in fine stone villas on the outskirts of the hardscrabble hamlets where, 40, 50 or 60 years earlier, they had been born and raised.

But in the coal patches of western Pennsylvania they lived together, Europeans from north, south, east and west of the continent, in detached clapboard wooden houses which were 'poorly built and were hot in the summer and cold in the winter'. Early in the twenty-first century Mary Elaine Lozosky wrote her memoirs and history of her typical coal patch home-town. Daisytown was a late-nineteenth-century mining settlement in West Pike Run, 30 miles south of Pittsburgh. At the beginning of the twentieth century, Lozosky calculated, there were 156 heads of household in Daisytown. Forty-eight of them, or 28.4 per cent, were Slovaks. Thirty-four were Hungarians. Fifteen were Poles. Fourteen were Finnish. Eight were Italian. The remaining 37 heads of household – less than a quarter of the patch's total population – were 'Anglo-American'. They all shared a life in Daisytown.

The Pennsylvania industrial historian Harold Aurand comments that:

The design of company houses varied over time, as employees added rooms and porches to the buildings, but the mode of construction remained the same until the twentieth century. The homes were put up quickly and inexpensively. Standard construction consisted of rough boards and batten sides on a wooden frame. Many had plastered interiors, but some had only wallpaper or muslin covering on the interior walls. Cellars were simple dugouts. Many homes stood on pillars above the ground. The cook stove served as the only source of heat during the winter. In summer the stove was carried to a nearby shanty to relieve the house of its heat . . .'

Company towns were drab. Streets were unpaved, boardwalks, if existent, were cracked, broken or rotten . . . All homes had vault-type outhouses, which were infrequently cleaned. Irregularly placed hydrants provided water.

Colder in winter and hotter in summer than they had ever been before, their dignity if not their actual persons always threatened by the Yellow Dogs, working for less money and with much less freedom than they had hoped, the family nonetheless played their small part in the creation of a new, multi-national mining community. The early coal patch settlements were a Babel of different languages and a kaleidoscope of different habits and traditions. They were made tolerable and even happy by the kindness of strangers and the decency of ordinary people. The totality of what they had in common dwarfed their linguistic and confessional differences. 'The remarkable thing about those mine patches,' recalled one man, 'was the fellowship and brotherhood that existed among the people. There was never any discrimination because of ethnic background or wealth or poverty or anything of that kind, everybody was for everybody, and it was really remarkable.' 'If you were in want for anything,' said another, 'a loaf of bread, a piece of bread, you know they'd give it to you. I can tell you that there was nobody in want. Anybody got sick, your neighbours came in to see if you wanted something, colored people, white people, made no difference what religion you were or anything . . .'

As the colliery working lives of Miles and Christopher, Thomas, Tom and James differed only in small degree and nuance from their earlier days in England, so did the domestic working life of Rosina Hutchinson. She may have learned that another name for parsley was petrushka and she may have been introduced to a diet rich in homegrown beans and celery, but otherwise her kitchen garden was familiar, poultry and rabbits were no strangers, and 'they spent a good deal of time gathering fruits, nuts, berries and mushrooms from the surrounding hills'.

Young William Hutchinson had an ordinary infancy there. Standing in the doorway of his company house, dressed in rough but clean homemade pants and smock. Watching with ambivalent eyes the older children – including his cousin Eliza McCormack – play socky ball (crude baseball with compressed old socks), caddy (a square chunk of wood numbered like a large dice with scores), hoops (preferably taken from the metal banding of an old barrel) or simply sliding down the ash dump on strips of tin. He stood there gazing at them, this brown-eyed child, absorbing the activity, waiting to grow up.

It may have been almost too familiar. They had come to see the elephant jump the fence, but there was nothing yet in North America sufficiently momentous or inspiring to justify leaving the ordinary comforts of home and crossing a quarter of the earth. The New World was turning out to be a tangential version of the Old. The Pennsylvanian coal patch was Billy Row on a different axis. In such vaguely frustrating circumstances, in a mildly troubled state of mind, Rosina Hutchinson – who knew herself to be confined to the relative security of the company house at least until the birth of her second child – addressed her family's other serious challenge in the United States of America.

It would not take long for four or five sober and industrious working men with small families to save the money necessary to approach once again the subject of Kate Wilkinson's blindness. They had a lot of options. They may have begun with one of the cheaper possibilities . . .

Upon receipt of $10 the New York and London Electric Association would have posted to Kate Wilkinson from Kansas City its 'Actina' device.

The Actina was a wonderful little thing. It was shaped like one half of a pair of opera glasses and was claimed to cure both blindness and deafness as well as a number of other complaints. 'It is,' said one dubious recipient, 'a small steel vial with screw stoppers at both ends. One end [the thicker one] cures eye ailments and the other [the thinner one] ear troubles. I live in hopes of seeing the Actina concern give a test, applying Blind Mary to one end and a deaf-mute to the other, and curing both at one stroke of business for five dollars apiece.'

Such sceptics notwithstanding the Actina enjoyed healthy sales in America at the end of the nineteenth century and into the twentieth. It had been developed and marketed by a certain 'Professor' (his academic qualifications were non-existent) William C. Wilson, an evangelical pastor from Kentucky. Wilson's religious affiliations lent the Actina respectability in some quarters. In August 1893 the Baptist Elder Sylvester Hassell of North Carolina encountered the Actina at the World's Fair in Chicago.

Hassell was impressed by the World's Fair itself – 'no doubt the most magnificent collection ever made of the natural glories of the world, many of the innumerable and wonderful works of God, and many specimens and works of His greatest earthly creature, man.'

He was especially impressed, Hassell informed readers of *The Gospel Messenger*, by

. . . the department of Medical Electricity at the Exposition. As is well known by intelligent and well-informed physicians, electricity, which very closely resembles life, is of great value for rapidly curing or relieving both acute and chronic diseases which seem beyond the reach of medicine, especially pain, weakness, and affections of the nerves, sleeplessness, diseases of the eye, ear, head, throat, lungs, heart, spine, liver, stomach, uterus, bowels, and kidneys, and for painless and bloodless surgical operations.

Among the electro-medical appliances that I found at the Exposition, used and recommended by physicians, were Dr H.P. Pratt's Pocket Electrical Battery and inhaler (for headache, toothache, earache, neuralgia, nausea, eczema, la grippe, catarrh, deafness, asthma, and insomnia – sold for $5 by the Pratt Electro

Medical Supply Co., Room 610, Masonic Temple, Chicago, Ills., who make also, for physicians and patients, nearly all other electro-medical appliances); and Dr A. Owen's Electric Belts and Appliances (for the cure or relief of nearly all diseases – sold for from $6 to $30, by the Owen Electric Belt and Appliance Co, 201 State street, Chicago, Ills.)

And I found, in use and in great esteem, among some Primitive Baptist ministers' families in Indiana, Prof. Wm. C. Wilson's Actina (Pocket Battery) a generator of ozone, the most powerful and purifying of gases (an instrument both chemical and electrical – for all diseases of the eye, ear, throat, and head, catarrh, hay fever, asthma, neuralgia, and bronchial troubles, and dispensing with the use of spectacles; sold for $10, by the New York and London Electric Association, 1021 Main street, Kansas City, Mo.); and Wilson's Magneto-Conservative Garments (for all diseases; claimed, with the Actina Battery, to have 500,000 patrons in Europe and America; sold at from $38.50 to $158.50 by the same Company). Descriptive circulars may be had of these parties, on application.

Elder Hassell's enthusiastic and detailed promotion of such products to his readers in *The Gospel Messenger* led a less innocent age to doubt both his and the publication's objectivity. William Wilson's New York and London Electric Association had certainly hit upon one answer to the chronic difficulty of peddling a cure for blindness. By despatching the Actina device through mail order, Wilson made sure that he would not be present and personally accountable if it failed to work.

Or rather, when it failed to work. The Actina was a hollow tube of metal with a large opening at one end and a small opening at the other. The large opening was to cover an afflicted eye; the smaller one to be inserted into a deaf ear. The Actina contained several foul-smelling substances. That was almost the full extent of its accomplishments, its popularity among 'some Primitive Baptist ministers' families in Indiana' notwithstanding.

Twenty years later, early in the twentieth century, the New

York investigative journalist Samuel Hopkins Adams could still obtain an Actina device in the post and write about it in *Collier's Weekly*.

'Actina,' reported Adams, 'is alleged to cure deafness and blindness, also catarrh, nervousness and a few pathological odds and ends of that sort. Its religious backers are the St Louis *Christian Advocate* and the *Central Baptist*. Its booklet is a weird jumble of pseudo-physiology and bad English.'

Adams then described the unfortunate first experience of Kate Wilkinson or anybody else who took delivery of an Actina parcel.

> The Actina, upon being unwrapped from the box in which it is mailed, comports itself like a decayed onion. It is worth the ten dollars to get away from the odor. 'Can be used by anyone with complete safety', says the advertisement, but I should regard it as extremely unsafe to offer it to a person with a weak stomach.
>
> Its principle ingredient is oil of mustard, an active poison, regarding which the United States Pharmacopeia prints this emphatic warning: 'Great caution should be exercised when smelling this oil.' So the 'perfect safety' guarantee is hardly sound. The Actina contains also oil of sassafras, representing presumably a brave but hopeless attempt to kill the inexpressible odor, and some alkaloid, possibly atrapin.
>
> So far as curing any genuine eye or ear disease is concerned, the sufferer might just as well – and with far greater safety – blow red pepper up his nose and get his sneeze cheaper than by sniffing at a ten-dollar evil smell. The whole contrivance costs probably about twenty-five cents to make.

Its 'evil smell' would have been part of the Actina's appeal to the infirm. Surely nothing quite so hideous could possibly be created and sold if it did not have magical properties? Similarly, small traces of mustard oil on the eyeball or the delicate aural membranes would have – at the very least – stung ferociously, just as any radical medicinal treatment would surely hurt in order to heal. An unquantifiable number of people with impaired eyesight or hearing in the United States will have felt a surge of hope as the Actina's mustard oil bit and the burning sensation kicked in. There is no record of any of them – even those with the suggestive faith of late-nineteenth-century Baptist ministers' families in Indiana – discovering the slightest sensory improvement before Actina was finally banned under the Pure Food and Drug Act of 1906.

But ten dollars was . . . just ten dollars. Less than a week's wage in the coal patch. Actina could almost be written off and forgotten as a small bad call in this crap-shoot of an adventure. It was certainly no reason to give up. The disappointment of working conditions and employment prospects in the United States of America – the signal absence of lush farms lying empty, ready and waiting to be claimed by Tom Wilkinson – can only have elevated the importance of finding a cure for his wife.

There would soon be other unpredictable, if not unimaginable, concerns to occupy the family in this new land. There would soon be necessary journeys which made the trip to western Pennsylvania look modest. America was far from finished with them. But for the moment a relatively quiet life and humdrum jobs allowed them to settle, look around and test the limits of American medical science. The Wilkinsons and Hutchinsons were encouraged in their efforts by the fact that Kate's blindness was not, and never had been, total. She was practically sightless. She could not be expected to negotiate unaided a strange neighbourhood or even an unfamiliar room; she could not hope to learn to read letters or identify numerals. She recognised people by their voice rather than their face. But her ability to distinguish one bright mass of colour from another was undiminished. She would delight and amaze visiting girls by rubbing the fabric of their frocks between her fingers and telling them what nice red dresses they had on today. She could recognise the difference between blue and yellow. There was ample reason for hope that Kate Wilkinson's extreme myopia could be, if not cured, at least improved by the proper treatment. They would try again.

There were, said Samuel Hopkins Adams, 'scores of petty fakers who flit from city to city doing a little business in eye lotions'. Their 'patented preparations' were usually either solutions of boracic acid or of cocaine (which was still legal in the 1880s). Sufficiently diluted, both could be applied as an antiseptic eyewash. Boracic acid's recommended safe solution was 1.5 per cent, or a single tablespoonful in a quart of sterilised water; cocaine in an equally mild dilute was deployed in the nineteenth century – and still occasionally would be in the twenty-first – as a local anaesthetic in lacrimal duct eye surgery. Insufficiently diluted, cocaine and boracic acid could make a short-sighted person blind and a blind person faint from agony.

Then there were brand-name products such as Murine. Murine's treatments for dry, tired, irritated and red eyes were still being marketed in the USA in the twenty-first century. A hundred years earlier the Murine company advertised an eye solution named Banene as being able to 'absorb' cataracts. Adams decided then that 'its claims are preposterous. It is merely a fairly good cleansing solution'. Banene would not last long upon the shelves. Too many people decided too quickly, with Samuel Hopkins Adams, that 'the man who attempts to "doctor" his own eye for anything more serious than ordinary irritation is running a risk. As for "absent treatment", there is just one kind of eye that can be successfully treated by mail, and that is a glass eye.'

Consultation was clearly needed. Kate Wilkinson required the personal attention of a qualified and trustworthy ophthalmic specialist. Luckily there were some about.

Oren Oneal did not begin to practise until Kate Wilkinson was no longer in need of his services, but he is an illustrative archetype . . .

Dr Oren Oneal of Chicago was an excommunicated member of the American Medical Association who, despite his dismissal from that body for 'unprofessional conduct', continued to advertise his services in many of the popular American magazines at the turn of the nineteenth century. (He also cheekily kept his old AMA certificate hanging on his consulting room wall.) His claims, like the man himself, were unqualified. He was in his own estimation 'the most successful oculist of modern times'. Readers of *MacLure's* and *Collier's* would find themselves gazing at a photograph of a plump and apparently gentle and intelligent man with a neat moustache and a dress collar. (Samuel Hopkins Adams, who met Oneal, said that he was 'a singularly agreeable and frank specimen of the genus Quack'.★)

Beside Dr Oneal's picture on the advertisement was printed in tasteful type the legend: 'How Much Would You Take for Your Eyes? Would You Sell Them at Any Price?' The answers plainly being: 'Nothing! No!', Oren Oneal's implication was that the reader should therefore be prepared to pay any price to improve or regain the use of his or her eyes. And this was where Dr Oren Oneal stepped in.

In short, Oren Oneal charged $50 to cure blindness. His advertisements in the *Christian Endeavor World* (the publication of a late nineteenth-century American Protestant mission which was to survive into the twenty-first century) told the faithful: 'How I Make the Blind See and Cure All Eye Diseases in Patient's Own Home Without the Knife'. The answer was Oneal's 'dissolvent method'.

'By this mild and harmless treatment,' he said, 'I have restored sight to thousands in all parts of the world. With it I have cured cataract, optic nerve paralysis, granulated lids, pannus, pterygium, glaucoma, conjection of the optic nerve, weak, watery eyes and all other eye diseases.'

A canny soul known to us only as Mrs Price wrote to Oren Oneal giving him details of her own incurable eye condition and asking if he could cure it. 'I find the trouble,' he diagnosed after

★ 'Quack' was yet another immigrant to the United States. The word derived from the early Dutch term 'quacksalver': a compound of 'quacken', to boast, and 'salver', to salve.

examining her letter, 'to be paralysis of the optic nerve. I have been especially successful in curing such troubles as yours. So positive am I that your case is curable and that you can be cured in a short time that I will promise to continue the treatment free of charge after five months.'

Mrs Price called Oneal's bluff by offering to deposit twice his normal fee, $100, in an account to be drawn upon by the doctor when she was cured. He rejected her offer 'with pained dignity'.

For every Mrs Price there were scores of what Samuel Hopkins Adams called 'the eternally hopeful, eternally credulous', and to a certain point they will have included the normally hard-headed family of Kate Wilkinson. Too much had been invested by that family for them not to explore every avenue. Sooner or later they would reject it all for what it was: so much eyewash. Within their own lifetimes, indeed, the United States legislature would sweep away most of the Oren Oneals and William C. Wilsons. But before that the American dream itself had to die within the hearts of the Hutchinsons and Wilkinsons, and their American dream did not die easily.

So the eye doctors continued to prosper. Dr W.O. Coffee built himself a sumptuous new mansion in Des Moines, Iowa, on the proceeds of his eye-and-ear infirmary and fraudulent mail-order cures. Dr P. Chester Madison established himself in Chicago, an overnight train journey from Pittsburgh, in the 1880s as 'America's Master Oculist'. The *Christian Century*, another religious publication which would survive for a further 100 years and more, extolled the success of Madison's 'Absorption Method' (more eyewash) on 'little Ethel Chapman'. Little Ethel had been presented to the editor of *Christian Century* and had told him how the good offices of P. Chester Madison had saved her from blindness. The editor was impressed. To hear little Ethel tell her tale of miraculous healing, he wrote, 're-minded one of the sweet song of the skylark soaring to greet the morning sun'.

We cannot know how many weeks' wages were posted from the western Pennsylvania coal patch to the likes of P. Chester

Madison, William Wilson and Oren Oneal. All we can know is that whatever money was spent, it was spent in vain. Disillusion will have seeped into the search. It would not yet end, but it would be interrupted. The quest to cure Kate's blindness would be distracted by an unforeseeable sub-plot. The journey of the Hutchinsons and Wilkinsons was diverted off the map.

THE UNKNOWN

For reasons that I suppose were linked to whatever residual shame or actual legal complications were threatened by Rosina's bigamous second marriage, neither my grandfather nor anybody else in the family was forthcoming about his years in the United States. At no point in my own childhood did anybody sit me down and tell me the whole round story. Fragments of the tale emerged piecemeal, chiefly from William's children: my aunts and my father.

Those fragments cropped up rarely and unpredictably. You had to keep an ear out for for them. At Christmas dinners or summer holiday reunions some choice morsel, dropped casually, almost thoughtlessly into the mix by an older relative, might at any time of day or night add a small but telling extra dimension to the romance. They walked to Liverpool, I was told. Wasn't that a long way to walk? Yes, but they walked everywhere. From Liverpool they sailed to Philadelphia. Murky, semi-contradictory fables surrounded that voyage, including one which insisted that my grandfather had been born at sea and was therefore arguably stateless. Again, I now suppose that falsehood to have emerged from the need to conceal the fact that a man who was known throughout his life as William Hutchinson had actually been born and christened William Hall.

They searched everywhere for cures for Great-aunt Kate's blindness. They went to Pittsburgh to labour in the western Pennsylvanian coalfield. A sister ran off with her Irishman to New Orleans and was never heard from again. They searched for her in vain and shortly presumed her to be dead, and presumed the Irishman to have been complicit in her death. Until the day of his death, into my own lifetime, my grandfather would never allow the colour green to be painted or displayed anywhere in his small pit cottage.

And then . . . then they went west, far west, to the places that we shall visit later in this narrative. They went from a relatively mundane unknown into an astonishing unknown. My imagination followed them there. It still does.

6

The Irish Channel

New Orleans, Louisiana, 1887

In the North one hears the [civil] war mentioned . . . but as a
distinct subject for talk, it has long ago been relieved of duty . . .
The case is very different in the South. There, every man you
meet was in the war; and every lady you meet saw the war. The
war is the great chief topic of conversation . . . It gives the
inexperienced stranger a better idea of what a vast and compre-
hensive calamity invasion is than he can ever get by reading books
at the fireside.

— *Mark Twain,* Life on the Mississippi *(1883)*

Rosina Hutchinson gave birth to a baby girl in western Pennsylvania. For reasons that will become clear we do not know
what she was named. But we can make an informed guess. She is
likely to have been called after Rosina's mother and the older
sister who had loyally witnessed Rosina's bigamous marriage to
Miles. She is likely to have been christened Elizabeth Hutchinson.

William's baby sister, the first genetic offspring if not the
first acknowledged child of Miles and Rosina, would have
been a precious creature. Baby Elizabeth Hutchinson might
even have provided a reason for them to settle and stay on the
coal patch. The infant could have curbed Miles' itinerant
instincts, as time would eventually show that they could
indeed be curbed.

But Elizabeth Hutchinson, through no fault of her own, was
not given the opportunity to work as a drag-anchor on her father
and mother. There was a quartet of young families in this

travelling clan. Three of them, the Wilkinsons, Halls and Hutchinsons, were reasonably happy units. The fourth, the McCormacks, was not.

James McCormack may have been unhappy in the company of his wife's sisters and their husbands. He may have been unhappy with his wife Rachel herself – he had after all travelled at first to America without her. He may have been unhappy about returning to his old life as a coalminer in the vast open spaces of the American continent. He could have been made unhappy by any or all or none of those things. He was certainly unhappy enough one day in 1886 or 1887 to rise up and inform everybody else that James, Rachel and young Eliza McCormack were packing up and leaving for New Orleans.

Nobody followed at first. New Orleans was so far away as to be unimaginable and the others had responsibilities still in Pennsylvania. But as the months passed following the departure of the McCormacks it became slowly, disturbingly clear that something ominous had occurred. James, Rachel and Eliza McCormack had, they knew through the US Mail service, arrived safely in New Orleans. But after a short period of time her few letters from the deep south ceased. Shortly after their cessation – as Rosina, Sarah and Kate found their mild irritation with the feckless Rachel turning into something tighter, harder and more painful to contemplate – other letters did begin to arrive from Rosina's family in County Durham. They contained distressing news. Rachel's husband James and daughter Eliza, the Hutchinsons were informed, had unexpectedly reappeared back home in England without her. Despite a series of frantic approaches from the Robson family, James McCormack would tell nobody in England what had become of Rachel.

There seemed to be one more railroad track to take. They did not have to take it. It was not a forced route-march. There was undoubtedly a pressing need to make some effort to trace the missing Rachel, but the Hutchinsons and Wilkinsons knew enough about the United States by now to realise that even if she was still alive, their chance of locating one lost young woman in the drifting mass of humanity on this epic sprawl of prairie, forest, desert and highland was too slim for anybody back home in Durham to comprehend.

They went nonetheless, and their reasons for going could have had more in common with the motives of James McCormack than they might have been prepared to admit. A period of time spent in a sleepy industrial hollow on the eastern outskirts of that boundless young country could actually encourage restlessness. There was something darkly seductive about those thousands of square miles of apparently empty land. Having come so far, why stop here? Whatever lay in the western future, it would be new. There would be more to see, more to do, more to discover and possibly more to achieve.

And there was now a missing sister to bring home. Miles, Rosina, William and Elizabeth Hutchinson, along with Tom and Kate Wilkinson, collected their things together, said goodbye to Thomas and Sarah Hall, Christopher Hutchinson and the coal patch, and made their way south to Louisiana. They were still in search of another life. They were still in search of a cure for blindness. They were also in search of Rosina and Kate's sister Rachel.

They boarded a train again. A tortuous journey lay ahead. They returned to Philadelphia and then travelled south to Louisiana down the eastern seaboard before branching south-west to the Gulf of Mexico. It was a distance of over 1,500 miles. Their travelling time, pulled by locomotives which averaged less than 30 miles per hour, which took lengthy halts at stations and which almost always deferred to freight, was three days and three nights. This was a passage made unusual not only by its staggering duration. An article in *Harper's Monthly* magazine in 1880 remarked,

> The differences between the methods and conditions of travelling by railroad in America and in England produce a marked impression upon the traveller from either country . . .
>
> The American railroad car consists of one compartment of the

entire length of the vehicle. The English railway carriage consists of several compartments of the width of the vehicle. This is the radical difference, as far as the traveller is concerned, between the two . . .

The American locomotive was certainly slower than its British equivalent, but according to this American magazine it had an

> . . . imposing splendor . . . its comfortable and lofty cab of oiled and polished wood, its gay brass bell, the soul-stirring whistle, the noble head-light and the cow-destroying pilot, the great cinder-consuming smoke-stack (unless it be a hard-coal burner, in which case that feature shrinks to moderate proportions), the powerful drivers and compact cylinders, the eccentric connecting rods, and all its parts radiant with the glitter of polished steel or burnished brass, or decked with appropriate vermilion or emerald green. In all of these matters the English locomotive compares with it much as a lawn-mower does with a New York fire-engine.

Despite the proud egalitarianism of the nation there were in the United States, as in the United Kingdom, three classes of carriage.

> The Englishman who travels in the United States . . . notices in American railroad travel the rapid growth of the class distinction, and the eagerness with which its conventional advantages are availed of by a constantly growing proportion of the public. It appears to him that the differences of the conditions of travel in the two countries are really very slight, and that the distinctions of a first, second, and third class exist already in America in no slight degree, and will, before the lapse of many years, be quite as emphatic and characteristic in America as they are in England.

The Hutchinsons and Wilkinsons travelled by the ordinary car, or third class –

well equipped, well ventilated, and comfortable . . . your original carrier's wagon or stage-coach, in which I am exposed to the danger of having to sit for some hours side by side with a common workman or person of very inferior social condition, an individual whose close companionship is as repugnant to me as I assert that it is repugnant to your cultivated and wealthy classes – that is your third-class, disguise the fact as you may.

Your second-class is the open saloon of your 'parlor' or 'chair' car. There I secure, by an extra payment, one of some twenty arm-chairs which are disposed on each side, and I make my journey without the danger of any disagreeable intrusion or propinquity.

Your first-class is easily attained in the exclusive seclusion which is afforded by one of the compartments in these parlor, palace, or chair cars – compartments which have room for two, four, or more persons, and in which I can travel under the very same conditions as those which I enjoy on an English railway.

I detect two differences. In England I am conspicuously labelled as a first-class passenger, whereas here [in the United States] I have the advantages of one without formal or ceremonial emphasis. In England I secure my exclusive compartment by a gratuity to the conductor or guard; here I effect it by paying the extra fares which the compartment I select would earn if all the seats in it were occupied. The latter is the more expensive expedient of the two, but it commends itself to my sense of right . . .'

In America smoking is out of the question except in the car which is known as the smoker, and in the smoking compartment of the parlor palace arrangement. The former does a good deal to discourage smoking on trains. It is almost invariably an indifferent car, poor in all its appointments, filthy, and ill-smelling. So foul is its atmosphere, especially in winter, that all cigars smoked in it taste and smell alike, and all badly. Then a large proportion of the people who are hardened enough to travel in the smoker are victims of the distressing habit of chewing, and it is unnecessary to

describe how effectively they contribute to the general abom-
ination. The English third-class carriage is a counterpart in many
respects of the American smoker.

And then there was the matter – of crucial importance to long-
distance travellers – of ventilation and heating. In America 'if all
the passengers were of one mind in respect to their preference of
Fahrenheit, it could be arranged comfortably enough; but that is
impossible, and in winter the golden mean of the management is
sought in heating the car to the highest possible point. The
consequence is that travel is rendered uncomfortable and un-
healthy, while in summer the distribution of discomfort is more
arbitrary.'

So they travelled in large, overheated railway cars, through the
interminable countryside and along the indifferent high streets of
America's towns and cities ('To an Englishman the spectacle of
an American train running through the middle of the street is
preposterous in the last degree, and it is undoubtedly wrong in
both theory and practice.'). For hour after steady hour they
travelled southwards. At a certain point early in their odyssey
they entered a defeated land; a country still aching and resentful
in the aftermath of post-bellum Reconstruction.

The American Civil War had ended just 20 years earlier. Its
700,000 military and civilian dead had long been buried but
its memories and other legacies had not. The Hutchinsons'
train crossed into the old Confederacy after passing through
Washington, traversing the northern state line of Virginia and
clattering through the centre of Richmond. Here, reflecting the
despondency of the rest of the countryside, the timetables and
the line and the railway cars themselves began to deteriorate.
Here the locomotive's cow-catcher and powerful headlight
came into their own – 'In the rude railroading of the primitive
South and West,' reported our *Harper's Monthly* correspondent,
'. . . [they are] invaluable.' Here the Yankee fondness of punc-
tuality began to degenerate. As one northern visitor to the
southern states noted in 1884,

The only way to be sure to catch a train is to go to the station immediately after breakfast and be pretty sure of waiting there until noon. I found the president of the [rail] road standing in front of the little office explaining to the expectant passengers why there had been no trains out that morning, and the gentleman who conducts a peanut and ginger-cake business in front of the station informed me confidentially that in his opinion the officers of the road, who are strangers [investors from elsewhere] . . . are only waiting to get money enough in their hands to make it worth their while to 'skip the town' . . .

But as white Virginians and southerners from other states boarded their car, the Hutchinsons and Wilkinsons encountered also, 20 years after its collapse, a remorseless nostalgia for the ante-bellum world of white mansions and white girls in white crinolines, white-owned plantations and black slavery. A sympathetic visitor to Virginia six years earlier, in 1881, commented,

The drift of their conversation is backward. They are full of reminiscences about the war, and living in a State clothed with battle-fields, it seems quite natural that this subject should be taken up . . . But it is not confined to such cases. Bourbons, talking with Bourbons* on the streets, in their houses, in public gatherings, converse more freely and with more zest about the lost cause than about any other topic under the sun.

To a traveller from the industrial north, Virginia in the 1880s was a stultified and insular place.

In Richmond your attention is proudly directed to the Capitol-square, which is regarded as one of the wonders of the continent.

---

* The traditional catch-all 'Bourbons' for the white and usually affluent citizens of this part of America stemmed from Bourbon County, which was originally formed within Virginia in 1786 but six years later became part of Kentucky. The county also loaned its name to the emblematic corn whiskey distilled and consumed throughout the southern states.

It is a pleasant little grass-covered hill, well-shaded, with tame
gray squirrels running about the lawns and winking at you from
the trees as you pass near them. But the Capitol is found to be an
extremely dingy affair, and the rooms in which the Legislature
meet are so barely furnished and so dirty that none but a Southern
Legislature would occupy them.

In Staunton they brag of their town, and yet it is a place of
narrow streets, lined with two-storied gable-roofed buildings,
some of brick and some of wood, the pavements are mother
Virginia soil, and the sidewalks are sometimes paved and sometimes without pavements . . .

Lynchburg's vaunted wealth was hardly in evidence aside from
the quality of its public schools, which was apparently owed to a
small and singular campaign of political assertiveness by the
newly freed and enfranchised black population of the district.
If so, it was an initiative for which Virginia's blacks would get few
thanks from Virginia's whites. 'The motto of the State should be
"Virginia for the Virginians", and the white Virginians at
that . . .'

The Hutchinsons, along with our traveller from 1881, cannot
have failed to have 'talked with some of those men who admit
that all talk about paying the debt [owed to the Federal US
Government] is bosh, that all pretence of favoring honest
elections is hypocrisy, and that the talk about equal rights for
anybody but white men is humbug pure and simple. There is no
regret or shame felt at the ballot-box stuffing outrages on the
blacks. They are justified still as a necessity to prevent "nigger
domination".'

Forty-two per cent of Virginia's population at that time was
African-American. In 'free, democratic' elections the state returned no black congressmen, no black senators and on average
only 25 per cent of state legislators were 'colored'. Could the
family from England have met in their railway car, along with the
unrepentant white supremacists, 'a young man from Virginia
University . . . who said that he had always doubted the truth of

the statements about violence to negroes to prevent them from voting, says he has been convinced by what he heard there that the stories are true, and he has heard from eye-witnesses of, or participants in, them that they were cruel and unjustifiable'?

Perhaps the Hutchinsons and Wilkinsons heard by 1887, as did another visitor to the troubled south in that year, voices of regeneration. Perhaps a man told them also that 'We have allus been a-making tobacco yer . . . yes, we've allus been a-making it, but now we air a-manufacterin' it.' Perhaps they were shown through the railcar window the 'new tobacco factories . . . new cotton mills send more wheels whirling, and flour is being ground out . . .' Perhaps they also noticed, like a censorious northerner, that in contrast to the hubbub of Philadelphia and Pittsburgh,

> it is not hard to find an abundance of loafers in the streets still, nursing corner groceries, generously mixing statesmanship, weather and tobacco juice, and growing stoop-shouldered together in ardent efforts to put their fingers through saggy pantaloons pockets . . . [but] this army of do-nothings has lessened materially since new temptations to industry have come in the form of competing manufacturers offering wages hitherto only heard of in reports from a distance . . . Soapstone and slate quarries, cotton cloth making and other industries on a modest scale are paying for labor and making things generally better for the poor man, white and black.

Could they have watched and listened and absorbed such things? Did they notice and wonder at and discuss the grudging segregation between their white and black fellow passengers as their train rolled into the warm south? Or did they close in among themselves, strangers in a strange land with their own private mission to protect?

Finally their locomotive inched through the Louisiana wetlands, over creeks and swamps, past profuse tropical vegetation. Strange exotic birds fluttered out of the dripping emerald trees.

They passed ramshackle villas flying Confederate flags. They passed long, narrow rectangular cabins, built from the timbers of small cargo vessels which had made a one-way voyage down the Mississippi River. They passed inland an enormous body of still water. They entered New Orleans.

William Hutchinson was in that year of 1887 approaching his fifth birthday. Some 15 years later another young boy was taken by his grandfather to New Orleans for the first time. In adulthood he would recall the experience. If the city on the gulf was strange and tantalising to Lyle Saxon, who had come from an upcountry Louisiana plantation, to William Hutchinson from Durham and the western Pennsylvania coal patch it was like passing through the portal of another world. Nothing will have prepared his senses of smell, hearing and sight for the experience. His skin will never have been bathed in such humid heat. The sheer variety of humanity, half of the world's people clustered in a few square miles, will have made him flustered and amazed. Even the ground beneath his feet was warm, damp and precarious . . .

> The uneven cobblestones make it difficult for him to walk sedately . . . he slips and stumbles instead. As they approach the market he looks curiously at the squat, slate-covered roof supported by tapering pillars of masonry. Under the arcade he sees a moving mass of men, and the building buzzes like a hive of bees.
>
> Wagons pass by, creaking under the weight of cabbages, of carrots, lettuce, of red and shiny tomatoes. Drivers shout and beat their horses. Whips crack. Men and women line the curb, bargaining with those who sell vegetables and other produce. Old negro women with bright-striped *tignons* on their heads and with baskets on their arms, wander about buying a little of this and a little of that. Fruit is piled high; globes of color, red, green, orange and clusters of purple grapes. Two nuns, wearing dull blue robes and stiff white head-dresses, are buying a bunch of bananas.

A negro man passes bearing upon his head a flat basket filled with pink roses; the basket bobs in the air above the crowd, and the man whistles as he goes by, a trill of clear, liquid notes.

An old Indian woman, wrapped in a blanket, is selling baskets striped red and green; and near her two Italian children crouch beside a pillar of crumbling masonry warming their hands over a charcoal furnace. A lean black dog runs by with a piece of raw beef in its mouth, and a yellow cat with a little bell at its throat puts up its back and hisses like a snake . . .'

The boy hears the rapid trilling of French, the soft slur of Italian, and the easy droning of negroes' voices. It is all new and strange and delightful.

This township had been built on a loop – a crescent of land, which made one of its earliest English-language nicknames the Crescent City – at the very foot of the Mississippi River. Steamboats and pleasure yachts cruised its warm waters; trading vessels arrived from all over South America, the Caribbean and Europe. It was a vivid collage of people, languages and activities. It was a city of cemeteries (40 of them) and brothels (probably several hundred). It was a piratical tropical playground, a little bit of eighteenth-century Latin America or the French West Indies, some of whose citizens were in the 1880s attempting – with varying degrees of success – to transform into a responsible, respectable, presentable modern American town.

There were two New Orleans. They co-existed – they even merged. But as adults, if not children, would distinguish only too clearly, there were two of them. There was the tumbledown, feckless, artlessly gorgeous New Orleans described one Sunday morning in 1887 by Charles Dudley Warner, where,

In the balconies and on the mouldering window-ledges flowers bloomed, and in the decaying courts climbing-roses mingled their perfume with the orange; the shops were open; ladies tripped along from early mass to early market; there was a twittering in

the square and in the sweet old gardens; caged birds sang and sang
the songs of South America and the tropics; the language heard
on all sides was French . . .

This city, this New Orleans, had been a colony of both France
and Spain before the Louisiana Purchase took it into the United
States in 1803. By the 1880s its most celebrated people, what
could be termed the signature population of New Orleans,
whether white or black or mulatto, spoke a French Creole★
dialect and lived largely inside Spanish Caribbean architecture.
Their political as well as social and cultural influence was still
strong – in 1887 the Mayor of New Orleans, J. Valsin Guillotte,
was a Creole. Those were the people who would synthesise a
unique cuisine and at least two forms of singular music – cajun
and jazz – from their environment and their kaleidoscopic
heritage.

Their spiritual if not always actual home was in a rough and
untidy square half-mile known as the Vieux Carré, the old centre
of New Orleans which would later be celebrated as the French
Quarter. The latter was not entirely a misnomer. Throughout
the nineteenth century it continued to be a Creole French-
speaking neighbourhood, although its houses had been rebuilt in
Spanish colonial vernacular following two disastrous fires in the
late eighteenth century. This Spanish influence had gifted to the
Vieux Carré its trademark wrap-around wrought-iron balconies
and cloistered inner yards, some a starburst of orange, lemon and

★ According to the *Encyclopedia of Cajun Culture*, the term 'Creole' originally
derived from the Portuguese 'crioulo', a slave of African descent; gradually it
came to describe all colonists living along the Gulf Coast, especially in
Louisiana, and by the nineteenth century was used by black, white and
mixed-race Louisianans to distinguish themselves from other settlers. Their
dialect, Louisiana Creole, developed from eighteenth-century French, simpli-
fying such words as quatre (four) and huit (eight) to 'kat' and 'wit'. Nous-autres
(we) had become 'nous-zot', and vois-toi plus tard (see you later) 'wa toi pli tar'.
It also incorporated Choctaw and other Native American terms, some Latin
from its Spanish period and English from the Anglo-Americans, and was of
course subtly infiltrated by the dialects of west and central Africa which had
been expatriated to Louisiana on board the slave hulks.

magnolia trees and other domesticated flora, others worn and rusted and insanitary slums.

The other New Orleans was a tense, frequently violent and only partly integrated city. When Mark Twain arrived in this 'metropolis of the south' in the early 1880s he found it to have discovered, chiefly through immigration, a new industrial energy:

> It is a driving place commercially, and has a great river, ocean, and railway business. At the date of our visit, it was the best lighted city in the Union, electrically speaking. The New Orleans electric lights were more numerous than those of New York, and very much better. One had this modified noonday not only in Canal and some neighboring chief streets, but all along a stretch of five miles of river frontage.
>
> There are good clubs in the city now – several of them but recently organized – and inviting modern-style pleasure resorts at West End and Spanish Fort. The telephone is everywhere. One of the most notable advances is in journalism. The newspapers, as I remember them, were not a striking feature. Now they are. Money is spent upon them with a free hand. They get the news, let it cost what it may. The editorial work is not hack-grinding, but literature.

By the 1880s the Cajun gumbo ingredients of French and African and Native American origin had been supplemented by other immigrations. Thousands of refugees had escaped civil unrest in Cuba. Germans had arrived in number. Greeks fled the Ottoman Empire. European Jews appeared in the streets. Sicilians had stepped onto the wharves. Mexican peons had walked north. Kentuckians ('Kaintucks') and other Anglo-Americans floated their longboats downstream on the Mississippi. And during and after the mid-century Great Famine in their home island the Irish had arrived in force. In the course of the nineteenth century the population of the city increased from 10,000 to almost 300,000. 'We come to look upon New Orleans somewhat as a small slice cut out of Paris,' wrote a visitor in 1884, 'but when we form any such idea we make a mistake . . . You hear a great deal of French talked in the streets by both blacks and whites, and it sounds odd enough to hear a coal-black porter or a half-clad newsboy chattering French like a Parisian.'

But the hucksters in the French market 'are mostly Germans' selling 'cabbages, turnips and such ordinary vegetables . . . Half the [sur]names on the [commercial] signs are American or Irish, and it rather breaks the charm of a real French quarter to find yourself among the O'Shaughnessys, Hennessys, and Smiths, but all these names are common enough in the French quarter of New Orleans'. Even in the cemeteries 'the inscriptions on many of the tombs show that the occupants came years ago from the French provinces, but a fair proportion of the names are German, Irish or American'.

The civic answer to this nineteenth-century influx had been to divide New Orleans into different quarters. The great broad central boulevard of Canal Street, with its four or five parallel streetcar tracks as well as lanes for private horse-drawn carriages, became a line of demarcation between the Vieux Carré and the homes and businesses of the various incomers. Canal Street, 'the Broadway of the south',★ thus became and remained a cultural no-man's-land separating the old holy ground of the entrenched Creoles and the briskly erected buildings of their new neighbours. 'Neutral ground', they called Canal Street, and neutral ground it would be.

The hunting ground of the Hutchinsons for sister Rachel lay just to the west of this neutral ground, within a stone's throw of the Vieux Carré. It was called the Irish Channel. Here, around a

★ The soubriquet reflected a certain southern complex about the rival north. Earlier in the nineteenth century it had been predicted that New Orleans could become the most powerful and wealthy city in the United States, but it was soon left far behind by such metropolises as New York, plaintively comparing its thoroughfares to the famous avenues of Manhattan, and later countering New York's 'Big Apple' status with its own cleverly insouciant 'Big Easy'.

church which had been dedicated to St Patrick in 1833 and in streets named after Sts Peter and Joseph, with their backs to the Mississippi River and their faces to the railway station, with one shoulder to the Vieux Carré and the other to the 'prairie palaces' of the city's affluent Garden District, Irish families settled. Their men built the city's drainage systems and worked as stevedores on the Mississippi docks. They lived in tenements and in terraces of simple single-storey 'shotgun' cabins, so called because it was theoretically possible to fire a bullet through the front door and straight out the back. They lived in a channel rather than a quarter because, unlike the sensible old parts of town, their low-lying streets – which stood no more than seven feet above the median high-water mark – became rivers when it rained.

There is no call to caricature the human produce of the Irish Channel and the rest of the Louisiana Hibernian diaspora. They included those O'Shaughnessys and Hennessys who became successful businessmen even in the Vieux Carré. They included Edmund McIlhenny, a banker who in 1868 blended mashed red *capsicum frutescens* peppers with white wine vinegar to produce a popular hot sauce labelled and sold as Tabasco. They included William J. Behan, a grocer who was Mayor of the city between 1882 and 1884. They included the nineteenth-century police chiefs Stephen O'Leary, Michael Kavanagh, John Burke, Thomas Boylan and David C. Hennessy, who was born in the middle of the Irish Channel in 1858 and was head of the city's police from 1888 until his notorious murder in 1890.

They included the father-and-son architectural team James Gallier (reputedly Frenchified from Gallagher) who raised many of the town's earliest and most impressive civic buildings. They included Margaret Haughery, who had been born in Ireland in 1813 or 1814, arrived in New Orleans in 1835, was widowed at a young age and devoted the rest of her life to the poor and the orphans of the city. They included many of the dedicated professional people who staffed and supported the John McDonogh public schools in the middle of the nineteenth century. They included, as they included throughout the English-speaking world, the forebears of some of the language's finest poets and authors. They included thousands of other decent and hard-working people whose lives have vanished from the memory and conscience of posterity.

The political presence and influence of the Louisiana Irish grew in size and confidence as the nineteenth century progressed. In 1830 the population of New Orleans was 46,000. Thirty years later, in 1860, after the main European and Anglo-American immigrations, the population had grown to 168,500 and it was estimated that 33,000 – or one fifth – of those citizens were Irish. By the 1880s, when the Hutchinsons arrived in search of the McCormacks, New Orleans had a population of 220,000 but the Irish proportion had fallen back. There were by then easily as many Irish people in New Orleans as there had been in 1860, but the abolition of slavery in the Louisiana countryside had caused an influx of African-Americans to the city. The Irish were still what they would continue to be: an extremely sizeable minority. They simply formed a smaller percentage of the ballooning population in 1880 than they had in 1860. They had been outflanked by the ebb and flow of ethnicities in this southern cauldron. But the Governor of Louisiana between 1881 and 1888 had been christened Samuel Douglas McEnery. The Irish still comprised a large and powerful enough section of America's twelfth city not only to elect one of their own to the highest office in the state, but also to offer a hundred thousand welcomes and a home away from home to men with the name of James McCormack.

New Orleans would never quite become a Boston or a New York. But the first St Patrick's Day in the city was celebrated as early as 1809. The Hibernia Bank was founded in 1870 and became the largest financial institution in Louisiana. By the 1880s New Orleans' Irish community was substantial, strong and organised. As the historian of immigration M. Mark Stolarik says,

> The Irish learned quickly enough how to function in an urban
> world. Irish priests, nuns and parishioners and Irish devotional

discipline gained the upper hand in the Catholic church, and Irish politicians and voters mastered the vagaries of New Orleans politics. In imposing a public order, the Irish literally policed the city – as priests in the parishes and police officers in the streets.

A manifestation of their confidence and self-esteem occurred in May 1886, when an 'immense mass meeting' of thousands of New Orleans Irish – there were no fewer than 300 prominent Irish-American citizens on the platform alone – delegated Governor McEnery to send a cable directly to the prime minister of the United Kingdom, William Gladstone, urging him to continue with his (subsequently defeated) efforts to establish home rule in the island of Ireland. The people of New Orleans, Gladstone was sternly informed, 'will watch the progress of this proposed legislation with great interest . . .'

All of those eminent persons, enterprises, devoted Catholics and energetic campaigns did not amount to a wholly unblemished community. It would always be difficult for a saint to clamber uncompromised through the American meritocracy. It would be doubly tough for an Irish saint in the multi-ethnic rough-house of mid-nineteenth-century New Orleans politics. The Louisiana Irish community as a whole developed more than a passing acquaintanceship with organised crime, official corruption and odorous white supremacist bodies. There is a credible suspicion that the martyred police chief David Hennessy, who was supposedly killed by the Sicilian Mafia, may have been more intimately involved with the New Orleans Irish mob than was desirable for a senior officer of the law. The brief mayoralty of William J. Behan would be celebrated for its financial idiosyncrasies.

It would be foolish to suppose that in the middle of the 1880s the Irish Channel of New Orleans, which Miles and Rosina Hutchinson and Tom and Kate Wilkinson entered in search of their missing sister Rachel, was anything but an unpredictable and occasionally deadly place. 'A rough neighbourhood,' Lyle Saxon remembered it during one of his childhood Mardi Gras, '. . . a neighbourhood of factories and corner saloons, but there was a carnival going on there, too. Here drunken men lay about in bar-rooms and many fights were in progress. Robert [the young Saxon's African-American escort] informed me that this was 'The Irish Channel' – a bad neighbourhood, and that 'White mens up thisaway would jes' as soon kill a nigger as eat dinner!'"*

The Hutchinsons had to take lodgings and walk into this quarter. The first would be easy; the second frustrating. Their quest was doomed before it began, and they knew it.

The prospect of physical violence would not discourage Miles Hutchinson and Tom Wilkinson (nor, apparently, did it much disturb Rosina). But a form of *omertà* operated in the Irish Channel. A Hibernian clannishness imported from across the Atlantic Ocean had been honed by the immigrants' collective urge to form a square against the rest of the unsympathetic world. It had been sharpened further by the defeat of their Confederacy in the Civil War, and brought to a fine edge by the secret societies formed after 1865 to resist 'Yankee carpetbaggers' and 'nigger supremacy'. It had been kept bright by a few precious decades of political, ecclesiastical and financial influence. Their stubborn suspicion of anybody – let alone an Englishman from the north – who came asking firm but unpleasant questions about someone named James McCormack was inevitable. The ease with which that suspicion could turn into hot-blooded hostility would make a coalminer from the Durham fields clench his fists and keep an eye on the exit.

---

* In making this assertion Robert had a certain amount of history on his side. Many New Orleans Irish, including the future mayor William Behan, had been members of a local proto-Ku Klux Klan white supremacist group called the Crescent White League. During post-Civil War Reconstruction in 1874 the Crescent League, motivated in part by the dilution of Irish influence in the city's constabulary, did battle with the newly established bi-racial police department. In an armed insurrection at the foot of Canal Street between 15 and 25 people were killed and more than 100 injured and President Ulysses Grant was obliged to send Federal troops to restore order.

Those questions must have been asked in the waterfront saloons. They were not frequented by genteel Louisianan society, but they established themselves in local legend. Mike Noud's Ocean Home tavern on Adele Street was the subject of an alternative explanation of the naming of the Irish Channel – seamen could see straight down through the buildings to its welcoming lights as they approached the docks. The Isle of Man saloon indicated the presence in New Orleans of another, smaller group of Gaelic immigrants from the shores of the Irish Sea. In McCauley's Tavern an Irish bartender named Martin Wilkes Heron had in 1874 discovered a sweeter and smoother way to get high than was usual with grain spirits. Heron added to his rough base alcohol 'An inch of vanilla bean, about a quarter of a lemon, half of a cinnamon stick, four cloves, a few cherries and an orange bit or two. He would let this soak for days. And right when he was ready to finish he would add this sweetener, he liked to use honey.' The resultant blend was then sold at McCauley's – and soon much further afield – as Southern Comfort.

The Bucket of Blood was – as the Hutchinsons would discover – one of many hostelries so named across the United States. At their most innocent they were so titled because, as one working man would explain, 'a bloody fight occurred there almost every day. Any meal might end in a knock-down-and-drag-out'. This rough-house tradition did not of course originate with the Irish. A visitor to New Orleans in 1806 related how after helping 'several times' to clear up bar-room brawls the French landlord told him: 'You make peace in my house – you tend bar – I give you boarding and $50 a month – you make peace.' The reputation lingered. When Margaret Mitchell, writing in the 1930s, needed to engineer the tragic death of a young French-American southerner in her Civil War novel *Gone With the Wind*, she seized on the device of having the man's lover receive – in the middle of the nineteenth century – 'a small package, addressed in a strange hand from New Orleans, a package containing a miniature of Ellen, which she flung to the floor with a cry, four letters in her own handwriting to Philippe Robillard, and a brief letter from a New Orleans priest, announcing the death of her cousin in a bar-room brawl.' Life, suggested Margaret Mitchell, was plainly as cheap as moonshine in those New Orleans saloons.

And often it was. Injury and death at the hands of drunken young men was not rare in nineteenth-century Europe. But upon arrival in the United States many of those nineteenth-century Europeans, suddenly unconstrained by the elders and the disciplines of their tight native societies and made giddy by the limitless skies of their new continent, created a sub-culture out of casual killing. The deaths, in New Orleans and elsewhere, contained elements in common. They generally had little motivation other than some hysterical catharsis; they usually featured alcohol; they often but not always were administered by firearms.

The bar-rooms of America in the 1880s were no place to court unpopularity. The Irish saloons of New Orleans in the 1880s were not places for Englishmen to ask leading questions about people called McCormack. The aggressive confidence of the New Orleans Irish would have shaken a Protestant family from England. It was not so much that the O'Shaughnessys and Hennessys of the Channel were more assertive than the O'Shaughnessys and Hennessys of County Durham. They were – but they were also more assertive than any other group of working people in County Durham. The Irish had come to realise the urban United States of America as their refuge of last resort. They were cornered there, and they would defend their corner to the death.

Rachel McCormack would not be found, as they must have known she would not be found. There were hundreds of McCormacks, MacCormacks and MacCormicks living in New Orleans in the 1880s. Who and where were they directed to? Whose doors did they knock upon? Did they turn uneasily, as people unaccustomed to asking favours, to Edward McCormack the grocer and his wife Rose on Gaiennie Street? Did they seek out the young deputy sheriff Hugh McCormick at his home in St Patrick's, to be met with mild sympathy and no useful information? Did they give up slowly or quickly, in unison or individually as the profitless days turned into weeks?

But Kate was still with them, and Kate was still in need. Just a few years earlier the blind author Mary L. Day Arms had visited New Orleans. The description that she left behind illustrates how Kate Wilkinson may have experienced the city, and the relationship that she had probably developed with her sighted sister Rosina: two women who had been girls together, who had grown up together and who had only briefly been separated since the day of Rosina's birth.

Although it was now the middle of January, flowery spring 'seemed lingering in the lap of winter'. The perfume of the violet, the scent of the rose, the gladness of the sun-beam and the brightness of the skies will ever linger in memory, while the geniality and goodness of its people will, in the 'dimness of distance,' glimmer like a soft love-light in the life of the blind girl.

I visited the French market, and drank a cup of the famed and fragrant Mocha; went to its cemeteries, which, in their flowery beauty, robbed death of its terrors; took a drive upon the shell road to Lake Pontchartrain; walked in Jackson Square; and, indeed, visited all localities of note in and around the city.

Should my curious readers wish to know how I could enjoy and describe all these, the answer will be found in my companion and friend, Hattie, who, with her wonderful adaptation and ingenuity, added to her remarkable descriptive powers, vividly pictured all to me, and, through an unwritten, indescribable language known only to ourselves, it became a system of mental telegraphy and soul language.

There is in Europe a blind man, whose name I cannot recall, who is led from Court to Court and from palace to palace by a frail young girl, and between these there exists the same mystic yet unerring language. What this little fairy is to him such was Hattie Hudson to me, or, to use the language of another:

'She was my sight;
The ocean to the river of my thoughts,
Which terminated all.'

Rosina, as Hattie to Kate Wilkinson's Mary Arms, would not give up on her sister's future. She would make another attempt in this miasmic city to allow Kate Wilkinson to see, rather than just hear and smell and have described by Rosina in that 'unwritten, indescribable language known only to ourselves' the peculiarities which surrounded her. Science – the science of electro-therapy, the Actina and Dr Oren Oneal – had failed them. It was perhaps time to take a chance on faith.

What were they like, those women? I recently met in County Durham one of the younger of Rosina Hutchinson's granddaughters. 'Yes, I knew my grandmother,' said Barbara. 'My grandfather Miles had died when I was a baby, but I knew my grandmother. She used to bring us down to stay with her, because my mother had three children in three years and the youngest one wasn't very fit. So my grandmother, Rosina, she used to bring my sister and me down to stay with her for days, to give my mother a break.

'She made all our clothes. We never had any bought clothes, she made coats and everything, all my dresses and my sister's dresses, and the little lad's trousers. A lot of old people then couldn't read or write but she was a good reader and a good writer. She had a good school to go to and she had a good stable family. The pitmen often saw to a good school and I think that's what happened, so she was well-read.

'She was very straight and very strict as well, there was no messing about with her at all. That was Rosina.'

I have in the past known more of Rosina's many grandchildren, but I did not think to ask them about her, and they were mostly the children of her oldest son William, and they are no longer around to answer my questions. So I have from those uncles and aunts only fragments, phrases like 'she was her own woman' and 'she didn't suffer fools', knowing code for the fact that, as Barbara suggests, it was not sensible to mess about with Rosina Hutchinson.

I did know another Rosina Hutchinson. She was my oldest aunt; my grandfather William's first daughter, whom he naturally named after his own mother. Her name was familiarly abbreviated to Ina. That Rosina Hutchinson, my Aunt Ina, was two generations younger than the heroine of this story. But she was born and bred in a Tyne and Wear pit village in the first decades of the twentieth century, which made similar demands on a girl as on those who were born and bred in a Tyne and Wear pit village just 40 years earlier.

I also suppose that it created similar young women. In which case, we may have known her equal but we will never meet her better. They were indeed 'very straight and very strict as well', those Rosinas. It would be easy to call them good, and in any worthwhile understanding of the term they were good women, but goodness was almost irrelevant in their lives. They were loving women, but love was also secondary – their love was taken for granted.

They were strong beyond ordinary measure. They occasionally saw their husbands, their brothers and even some of their sisters begin to weaken. In the face of what was in their world the only real disaster, untimely death, they sometimes saw others begin to fail. In the accurate realisation that if they too then faltered the centre would cease to hold and the nuclear family could fragment, they did not falter, not ever, not under any circumstances. Not for a visible flinching moment.

Not in public. Rosina Hutchinson – it does not matter which one – sought out a male relative with his despairing head in his hands after the funeral of his young wife. She spoke to him as if he were ten years old again. 'Think of your bairns' is an unsatisfactory summary of what she said at length. 'Sit up. Stand up. You have to carry on.'

He did carry on. We do not know Rosina's own emotions in the private hours that followed. She would not give posterity the satisfaction of recording them. Whatever they were, next day she set her face like stone against the world.

7

Nothing Exists But Mind

New Orleans, Louisiana 1887

The wonderful influence of imagination in the cure of diseases is well known. A motion of the hand, or a glance of the eye, will throw a weak and credulous patient into a fit; and a pill made of bread, if taken with sufficient faith, will operate a cure better than all the drugs in the pharmacopoeia.

– *Charles Mackay,* Memoirs of Extraordinary Popular Delusions and the Madness of Crowds *(1848)*

There were a good many faiths to choose from. It was a feature of those United States that a wide variety of Christian religious denominations affiliated themselves to physical healing with a commitment that, in post-Reformation Europe, was by the nineteenth century almost solely the province of the Roman Catholic Church. We have seen the attachment of Indiana's Primitive Baptist ministers to the miraculous ear-and-eye device Actina. Other spiritual messengers would broadcast their cures more loudly, across a wider distance and more persistently through the decades.

One of the most successful and long-lived of those movements sprang out of the soil of small-town New Hampshire in the 1860s. The middle-aged Mary Baker Eddy had become convinced that healing the sick and disabled was not only a feasible function of Christianity; it was its primary duty. At the age of 44 in 1866 Eddy suffered a fall and injured her spine. When she recovered she credited her devoted study of the Bible with her return to health. She had noticed in the New Testament that Jesus did not use nineteenth-century medical instruments, pharmaceuticals or expertise to heal the sick. Nor therefore, Mary Baker Eddy concluded, should she or anybody else:

> It is plain that God does not employ drugs or hygiene, nor provide them for human use; else Jesus would have recommended and employed them in his healing . . . The tender word and Christian encouragement of an invalid, pitiful patience with his fears and the removal of them, are better than hecatombs of gushing theories, stereotyped borrowed speeches, and the doling of arguments, which are but so many parodies on legitimate Christian Science, aflame with divine Love.

Christian Science took off in the United States. Between 1882 and 1889 Mary Baker Eddy passed on her beliefs to 800 students at her Massachusetts Metaphysical College in Boston. Those 800 apostles then fanned out across the nation, proselytising to such effect that just 20 years later Mark Twain could write:

> [Eddy] has launched a world-religion which has now six hundred and sixty-three churches, and she charters a new one every four days. When we do not know a person – and also when we do – we have to judge the size and nature of his achievements as compared with the achievements of others in his special line of business – there is no other way. Measured by this standard, it is thirteen hundred years since the world has produced anyone who could reach up to Mrs. Eddy's waistbelt.

Blindness was one of the afflictions which nineteenth-century Christian Scientists claimed to be able to cure. At a mass meeting in New York's Metropolitan Opera House in 1899 thousands of devotees heard a senior member of the Church, Carol Norton, declare:

> Christian Science has cured and is healing such diseases as locomotor ataxia, blindness, deafness, softening of the brain, paresis, Bright's disease of the kidneys, erysipelas and rheumatism,

floating kidneys, cancer, tumor, calcareous deposits in the joints, paralysis, and shaking palsy.

The confirmation of physicians regularly graduated from allopathic and homeopathic medical colleges of national import will be gladly furnished to any person honestly skeptical of this statement.

If Kate Wilkinson was tempted – as who would not be? – by this extraordinary catalogue of corrected complaints, thanks once again to Mark Twain we know roughly the nature of her treatment. While touring Europe in 1899 Twain fell off a cliff near Vienna and broke several bones in his arms and legs. His Austrian hosts recalled that a 'Christian Science doctor' from Boston who 'could cure anything' was summering nearby. She was called to Twain's bedside.

She was middle-aged, and large and bony, and erect, and had an austere face and a resolute jaw and a Roman beak and was a widow in the third degree, and her name was Fuller. I was eager to get to business and find relief, but she was distressingly deliberate. She unpinned and unhooked and uncoupled her upholsteries one by one, abolished the wrinkles with a flirt of her hand, and hung the articles up; peeled off her gloves and disposed of them, got a book out of her hand-bag, then drew a chair to the bedside, descended into it without hurry, and I hung out my tongue. She said, with pity but without passion:

'Return it to its receptacle. We deal with the mind only, not with its dumb servants.'

I could not offer my pulse, because the connection was broken; but she detected the apology before I could word it, and indicated by a negative tilt of her head that the pulse was another dumb servant that she had no use for. Then I thought I would tell her my symptoms and how I felt, so that she would understand the case; but that was another inconsequence, she did not need to know those things; moreover, my remark about how I felt was an abuse of language, a misapplication of terms.

'One does not feel,' she explained; 'there is no such thing as feeling: therefore, to speak of a non-existent thing as existent is a contradiction. Matter has no existence; nothing exists but mind; the mind cannot feel pain, it can only imagine it.'

'But if it hurts, just the same – '

'It doesn't. A thing which is unreal cannot exercise the functions of reality. Pain is unreal; hence, pain cannot hurt.'

. . . 'I am full of imaginary tortures,' I said, 'but I do not think I could be any more uncomfortable if they were real ones. What must I do to get rid of them?'

'There is no occasion to get rid of them since they do not exist. They are illusions propagated by matter, and matter has no existence; there is no such thing as matter.' . . .'

In her compassion she almost smiled. She would have smiled if there were any such thing as a smile.

Rosina Hutchinson and Kate Wilkinson may or may not have come away from a consultation with a Christian Scientist as Mark Twain responded to Mrs Fuller – 'Do they let her run at large, or do they tie her up?' Twain would reflect that,

Within the last quarter of a century, in America, several sects of curers have appeared under various names and have done notable things in the way of healing ailments without the use of medicines. There are the Mind Cure, the Faith Cure, the Prayer Cure, the Mental Science Cure, and the Christian Science Cure; and apparently they all do their miracles with the same old, powerful instrument – the patient's imagination.

Although many if not most of those healers requested money for their services (Twain claimed that Mrs Fuller billed him for a staggering $234, but on the understanding that 'Nothing exists but Mind' he gave her an imaginary cheque), some required no reward other than their patients' devotion to the cause or faith involved. And others did not even request that. They were, as Twain indicated, everywhere and unmissable. Some were comically impertinent even at the time. The heiress Tillie Smith took her niece Caroline Hulse to 'The Holy Ghost and Us Society' faith-curing community at Shiloh in Maine which had been founded by Reverend Frank Sanford. Young Caroline Hulse was going blind, probably from cataracts. When The Holy Ghost and Us Society failed to restore her vision the blame was heaped upon her rakish, affluent father, Cornelius N. Hulse, for 'not being as Christianlike as he ought to be, whereas the sins of the father are being visited upon the child . . .'

However, a decreasing – by the 1880s, rapidly decreasing – number of faith or miracle healers roamed the nineteenth-century United States like hickory holy men; ragged relics of the Middle Ages, seeking nothing for their services, but only some small metaphysical satisfaction. In the 1850s a Prussian immigrant named Loewendahl achieved a measure of fame for 'curing paralytics, blind, lame and neuralgic people, without medicine and most miraculously. His method is simply to pass his hand over the affected part of the body a few times . . .' Mr Loewendahl's case notes tell poignant stories of the infirm poor in a society where few people other than such a sympathetic visitor were prepared to offer them the smallest degree of help and hope. Loewendahl treated at least one blind man, a news-paper-seller called Youngs who had lost his vision ten years earlier. After Loewendahl had run his hands over Youngs' eyes, the paperman declared that he could 'see daylight' and had 'perfect faith in the belief that he will be entirely cured'.

Faith healers would continue to thrive for another century and more, and some were better organised if not more plausible than others. It is possible to imagine Kate and Thomas Wilkinson, with the sceptical but loyal support of her sister Rosina and despite the weary cynicism of an increasingly frustrated and instinctively agnostic Miles, attending a mass Faith and Prayer Cure gathering.

The Hutchinsons and the Wilkinsons had been baptised and married into the modest, unpretentious Church of England. It is inconceivable that at home in Britain they would have lent any credence or a moment of their time to the restorative claims of the scores of fundamentalist Protestant sects which proliferated in the United States of America.

But they were no longer at home in Britain. They were adrift in the USA. And in the USA in the 1880s those evangelical groups and their fantastic claims were simply too numerous and ultimately too seductive to ignore. What is more, they were – at least initially – free of charge. After the failure of magnetic healing, the Actina and P. Chester Madison's eyewash, what was there to lose?

See what Rosina Hutchinson will have read, and Kate Wilkinson will have heard . . .

Year after year they will have been told of large miracles and small. Of the harness-maker W.H. Bulkley, who in 1884 placed his hands on the head of the consumptive Miss Ellen Buehle. Miss Buehle had been so weak that she had to be carried to the altar of Mr Bulkley's Baptist Church. Following a few moments of prayer and contact with the harness-maker she rose to her feet, walked back to her pew and later declared herself to be 'entirely cured'.

Of the Baptist Reverend E.D. Simons, who told a large conference of ministers in 1885 that 'prayer helps recovery, and every physician will admit that something beyond himself says whether we shall live or die. The unbeliever calls it nature, but the Christian doctor freely admits that if God wills we should not recover then all his medicines are in vain. In this sense there is a "faith cure".'

Of a prayer meeting which was held in 1886 at the bedside of a Mr Hoerder in Janesville, Wisconsin. Hoerder had been pronounced by two physicians to be terminally ill. During the prayer meeting he announced that he was cured, got out of bed, dressed himself, walked around 'and was able to walk to church the next Sunday'.

Kate Wilkinson had no desire to walk to a Baptist Church. But she did wish to improve her myopia. As strangers and newcomers to the American communities in which they temporarily squatted, the Hutchinsons and Wilkinsons had no access to the intimate fireside prayer meetings which ministers and elders and congregationalists might provide to their own relatives and neighbours and co-worshippers. Kate Wilkinson's last best hope was to attend a mass outdoor faith cure gathering and there, among the halt and the lame and the thousands of devotees, throw down her disability at the feet of the man on the platform.

Many such gatherings took place in the United States in 1887 and 1888. Rosina Hutchinson and Kate Wilkinson will have found themselves among a multitude, either inside a huge marquee or upon vast arrays of benches before a tabernacle. They were strong, determined and sceptical women. They had spent two short lifetimes reinforcing each other. They would not have been intimidated.

From out of the buzz of small devotional services which surrounded them, as that summer morning in 1888 passed towards a warm and sunny noon, there will have emerged such a man as Brother M.D. Hancox of the Faith Cure Church of the First Born. All of the functioning eyes and ears in the large assembly turned to the 'frail and devout-looking' Brother Hancox as he spoke first of Sister Juliette Ware, a mainstay of the Faith Cure Church who had in her time been cured by prayer of consumption, a fractured limb and three times of pneumonia, but who had recently died of 'a slight cold'. Brother Hancox had been privy to the intimacies of Sister Juliette's passing – 'Three times did her spirit leave her body and warn her of her time of departure. She saw seven tiers of angels all waving their wings . . .'

M.D. Hancox then confessed to his own squalid history.

Why, brothers and sisters, look at me and believe me that I was once a club man, vice-president of a big steamboat company and part-owner of a bank. I was a bold, bad man . . . who used to drive fast horses down this very road and then go to my home under the influence of liquor, and used to play a game of cards known as draw poker and then take the name of the Lord in vain, even I, because I had faith, was redeemed. But this was 20 years ago. Why, then I used to dance – dance the german.* Look at me now! How happy I am! I don't dance now.

Brother Hancox then called forward witnesses to the power of faith. Mrs John Leavens and Mr Benjamin Wetherill each announced to the masses that they had been cured of heart disease. Banjo Bill 'related his struggle with the curse of rum and of his supreme victory'.

And then the sick and infirm were called. A silence would fall across the meadow. They would kneel at the altar rail. They would whisper their disability to Brother Hancox, who would broadcast it loudly to the field. He would anoint them by laying his hands upon their heads. He would ask them to pray, and ask the gathering to pray with them, and he would mutter prayers himself.

He would lift his hands from their heads, and the bent would stand up straight, and the lame would walk around, and the deaf would cup their hands to their ears, and the blind would claim to see a light, and the thousands of joyful witnesses would erupt in hallelujahs . . .'

If Kate Wilkinson was among those kneeling at the tabernacle, even if she was among those briefly elevated by the mass euphoria, she did not walk away from the marquee and the wooden benches, the scraps of paper and picnic food, the hubbub and the trodden earth, away from the Faith Cure Church of the First Born, with 20/20 vision.

She would wake the next morning and open her eyes to the abstract block of vague colour which, by then, she realised would never be improved.

---

* The 'german' in which Brother Hancox once indulged himself was of course another immigrant, originally a French group dance called the cotillion, forerunner in the United States of the square dance.

I thought I saw them, not in Amish country on a train between Philadelphia and Pittsburgh, but in El Paso.

I stumbled into that western Texan outpost unprepared. I knew of course that it is on the Rio Grande. I knew that it is a cornerstone between two states – Texas and New Mexico – and two countries – the USA and Mexico. I knew that its name is hardly Anglo-Saxon in origin. But I stupidly did not expect El Paso to be quite so Hispanic.

How were immigrants defined in the 1880s? The term has always been highly nuanced, and its application has always depended upon where its subjects came from, and why. Different linguistic and ethnic groups are traditionally given a more reluctant welcome than cousins who speak the same language. So Polish and Bulgarian workers were considered to be aliens in the Pennsylvanian mines. Aliens whose labour was embraced and vigorously exploited, but aliens nonetheless – people who, once their contribution to industrial growth was finished, the majority of the region's politicial officers and possibly a majority of their English-speaking neighbours would have been happy to see go home again. Which is partly why so many of them did.

Money also plays a part. Immigrants looking for money are generally unwelcome. Immigrants bringing money, wherever they were born, whichever languages they can and cannot speak and whatever the shade of their skin, can scoot through customs.

The size of the welcome mat rolled out to immigrants, to the United States or anywhere else, in the 1880s or anytime else, is therefore quantifiable. The biggest, reddest and richest will be offered to a speaker of the same language who is of the majority ethnic group, and who is also a millionaire.

A slightly smaller but still thick and colourful carpet would be laid before an equally rich person who unfortunately had not (yet) a word of English. No Prussian baron was ever turned away from the Delaware wharves. A modest if somewhat worn rug was also thrown at the feet of such as Miles and Rosina Hutchinson, by virtue of their being white, Protestant, north-western European and speaking the official national language. Their financial deficit could be politely overlooked.

The rest either had no welcome mat at all, or had the rug pulled out from under them. It is feasible that a penniless blind woman such as Kate Wilkinson would have been turned away from the United States in 1884 if she had been a penniless blind Roman Catholic woman from Sicily who did not speak English. Those who were admitted went quickly to the foot of a sliding scale of swarthiness and need. At the bottom they were dispensable and treated as such. A step or two up they could be used, but reluctantly and resentfully.

There may in the early twenty-first century be three-quarters of a million people living in the El Paso metropolitan area of the United States of America. Fewer than 10 per cent of them are whites of northern European origin. More than 80 per cent of them are of Latin origin, whose ancestors inhabited this region long before the English speakers.

So I made a big mistake in El Paso. Boarding a bus north to Albuquerque alongside several dozen speakers of Mexican Spanish, I saw a small family group. It consisted of four adults in their 20s or 30s and a couple of children. They held together in the throng, the children corralled in the womens' full skirts while the men looked out alertly. One of them caught my eye, sized me up in an instant, dismissed me as safe and turned away again.

This is them, I thought. Hard-working adults and their bright children, on the long road to a better life. But it wasn't them at all. I had not realised that I was in a place where the word 'immigrant' loses all of its meanings but one. The word ceases there to have any legitimate historical, social, economic or moral application. Its only remaining use, a perverted use, is political. If there was an alien in that crowd, his name was Hutchinson. That much has not changed since the 1880s.

8

The Painted Desert

Arizona, 1888

In regard to the Zunis and Moquis it is now asked, 'Are they Aztec, Toltec, or what?' . . . What a turning upside down of institutions of a civilized, cultivated and refined people, who are now forgotten and almost obliterated by the lapse of time. A people, perhaps, scientific in the extreme, and whose institutions in many respects equalled, if not excelled, some of those of our own civilization.

– *Enoch Conklin,* Picturesque Arizona *(1877)*

Some 225 million years before the small family unit of Hutchinsons and Wilkinsons arrived there from New Orleans in 1888, in the Late Triassic Age, the region which would one day become north-eastern Arizona in the United States of America lay on the equator.

It was a tropical landscape. Rivers and streams irrigated its lowlands; ferns proliferated on their banks. Lungfish, clams, freshwater sharks and crabs inhabited the warm waterways. Small herbivorous and carnivorous dinosaurs up to 15 feet in length crept and strode through its undergrowth. Large proto-crocodiles preyed on fish and other reptiles.

Most relevantly to this story, it was forested with gigantic, towering coniferous trees as much as nine feet in diameter and 200 feet high. As trees will, many of those behemoths collapsed – washed away at the root by rivers, undermined by insects, rotted by damp. Some lay where they fell, others broke up and were carried downstream by seasonal floods. Some – probably most – decomposed. But others fossilised.

Fossilised trees and other vegetation are common phenomena, in North America and elsewhere. But a strange if not entirely unique process affected the trees which died in north-eastern Arizona as the continental plates shifted and the land moved north and the equatorial forest turned slowly, imperceptibly, into an arid desert.

The ash from volcanoes erupting to the west of the dying jungle was carried by the wind to this coniferous cemetery. Silicon dioxide and other chemicals present in the volcanic ash dissolved in the marshwater and soaked into the fallen wood. A petrification process then began which over the centuries not only preserved the logs in exquisite stony detail, like a scrapyard of tree-trunks sculpted by Michelangelo, but also created at their centre crystals of such semi-precious stones and minerals as clear and milky quartz, purple amethyst and yellow citrine.

Mining for such stones and metals in the dry, shallow earth drew Europeans into this part of Arizona. The extraordinary psychedelic colours, the pale orange, yellow, blue, violet, gold and red hues which carpet the buttes, mesas and hardened dunes led the first Spanish colonisers to christen it 'el Desierto Pintado' – the Painted Desert. To a northerner with more experience of industrial landscapes it looked, promisingly, like a massive seepage of chemical waste. Such an immigrant would know intuitively that wherever such seepage occurred, there was a valuable wellspring to be found.

Those men had hiked west before Arizona and its surrounding territories became part of the United States. The whole wide district had been a Spanish colony since the sixteenth century. It was then part of independent Mexico until the United States army occupied Mexico City during the Mexican–American War of 1846–48, and the Republic of Mexico was obliged to cede its territories of Alta California and Santa Fé de Nuevo México to the United States, in whose dominion they became California, New Mexico, Texas and Arizona.★

★ Before 1848 Alta California and Santa Fé de Nuevo México had composed more than half of the entire land area of Mexico. That is why in Mexico the 1846–48 war has never been known by such an equivocal term as the Mexican–American War. It is called La Intervención Norteamericana – the North American Invasion.

Just a few years later, in the 1850s, a middle-aged freebooter and trained surveyor named Jacob Snively struck gold near the Yuma Crossing in western Arizona, where the Gila tributary runs into the great Colorado River. A short-lived boom town emerged on the spot (Gila City had 1,200 residents in the late 1850s. In 1877 a traveller encountered there only 'the hotel keeper and his son – two, a man to attend to the stage horses – one, an Indian squaw, boy and papoose – three, three dogs – three. Making in all nine living beings'). Strikes of silver and – most permanently and profitably – copper followed the gold rush, effectively uninterrupted by the Civil War, which paralysed the eastern states during the 1860s but which – despite Arizona being claimed as part of the Confederacy – produced only a few minor skirmishes and a handful of fatalities in the Great American Desert.

Within a few short years Arizona was bristling with white miners. According to the official census, in 1860 the population of the territory (it would not become an autonomous state until 1912) was 6,500 people. The census recorded only those citizens of Hispanic and other European origins, who were chiefly resident in the mining camps and in such small suburban enclaves as Tucson and Phoenix. The Hopi, Navajo, Apache, Pimo, Maricopa, Papago, Zuni, Moqui and other Native American peoples – who were largely uncounted but who must have numbered tens of thousands – did not feature in the census unless they occupied some position within a European household.★ Outside Phoenix, Tucson and such scattered, riotous enclaves as Gila City, and away from the east–west Gila Trail, hardly any European language was then heard in Arizona. For three centuries Hispanics had met, settled alongside, quarrelled with, attempted to convert, occasionally fought and frequently inter-married with the settled Native American people. Bilingualism was commonplace, but the main languages were Spanish and Navajo or Hopi.

★ Not until the Indian Citizenship Act of 1924 were all Native Americans accepted as enfranchised members of the United States polity.

Twenty years later, in 1880, the official population of Arizona Territory had increased six-fold to 40,440. Most of the extra 30,000 people were Europeans whose *lingua franca* was English. By 1890 the territory had almost 90,000 inhabitants. The Hopi/ Navajo/Hispanic hegemony was on the way to being submerged by gold-digging Europeans. It would never recover.

The Hutchinson and Wilkinson families, lately of County Durham, Philadelphia, Pittsburgh and New Orleans, formed a small fraction of those tens of thousands of invading Europeans.

They had failed, as they must have feared they would, to find Rachel McCormack. They had failed, as they must have guessed they might, to restore Kate Wilkinson's eyesight. They had found themselves farther than they ever intended to be from the faintly familiar north-eastern corridor of the United States. They had discovered that the hire-and-fire industries of that north-eastern corridor offered no easy route to affluence. They had trodden no sidewalks paved with gold; they had seen inequity and exploitation and much else that was reminiscent of their old, abandoned world. But in the very nature of the place they had also seen hints, thrilling glimpses, of its democratic possibilities. They knew most of all that they had barely scraped the coastline of America; that over there, beyond a hundred horizons, were promises that could not be denied by any European because no European had yet taken the trouble to discover if those promises were true. Could Miles Hutchinson ever sleep comfortably in County Durham if he was haunted by dreams of what might have been, troubled until death by visions of those unanswered promises?

They were still young. In 1888 the four adults lodging curiously in New Orleans – wondering idly, occasionally, how they ever came to be there – were in their 20s and early 30s. William Hutchinson was six years old and had never sensibly known a country other than America. His baby sister Elizabeth was in her second year. And Rosina was pregnant again.

They had sufficient time and energy to throw the dice once

more. Earlier in the nineteenth century a French Creole Louisiana landowner named Bernard Xavier Philippe de Marigny de Mandeville had, following a holiday in England, introduced to New Orleans a two-dice game which in London was called hazard, but which in the southern United States became known firstly as *crapaud*★ and later as craps. Among a dizzying number of quickly evolving scoring possibilities, craps basically called for two big throws: sevens (natural) and elevens (yo-leven, to distinguish the number's shouted syllables from those of seven).

There was no point in Miles and Rosina Hutchinson and Tom and Kate Wilkinson throwing an easy four or eight. There was no point in taking the train back north, unless it was to be the first stage of their journey back to England. There was no serious new life for them in Pittsburgh or Philadelphia, and probably no better prospects in New York, Boston or Chicago.

A big strike, a yo-leven was needed. It came as it must come on this continent, from 1,500 miles further west, from where the news emerged that European miners were digging not for company coal but for their own gold, silver, copper . . . and purple amethysts. Miles and Rosina and Tom and Kate took deep breaths, loaded their dice to throw elevens, and caught the transcontinental train on the Santa Fe route to the Petrified Forest in Arizona.

The Atchison, Topeka and Santa Fe Railroad had joined the Atlantic and Pacific Railroad to open a new line through the Arizona desert just seven years earlier, in 1881. Passenger trains began immediately to ply the line and a railroad station was opened at the small town of Holbrook in the Petrified Forest.

That was their destination. To reach it the party of four adults

---

★ The French word 'crapaud' means toad. Two schools of thought debate its original application to the game of craps. One suggests that Anglophones in New Orleans employed one of their milder nicknames for Frenchmen, Jean Crapaud, to describe a game that the French first introduced and played. The other proposes that the French themselves christened the game after the fact that its players crouched forward over the table like a congregation of toads. The former is more likely by a factor of several hundreds.

and two children entrained back north from New Orleans, probably travelling 700 miles to St Louis in Missouri. There they caught the westbound locomotive and steamed over 1,000 miles through Kansas and Colorado, down through New Mexico and into Arizona. The average speed of their trains on this entire odyssey was around 20 miles an hour.

The names of the halts – which they had ample time to notice – spelled out to them a story of the American west. They paused at the homesick settlements of Cuba and Lebanon. A few miles west of the small new town of Wichita in Kansas, which had been named after its native people, they stopped and stared with what can only have been a sense of amused wonder at the equally small and equally new town named Hutchinson, which was christened at its foundation in 1872 after a Vermont Baptist minister, teetotaller, Indian Agent, land developer, inveterate pioneer and vanishingly distant relative of Miles called Clinton Carter Hutchinson.★

They stopped at Dodge City, the Wickedest Town in the West, whose assistant city marshal ten years earlier had been a handsome thirty-year-old buffalo hunter called Wyatt Earp. Earp's deputy at the time was a dandyish gunfighter called Bartholomew 'Bat' Masterson and his constituents included the consumptive, alcoholic, hare-lipped dentist and killer John Henry 'Doc' Holliday. Their presence had been lively but short-lived. When the Hutchinson and Wilkinson families got in and out of Dodge in 1888 Earp was running gambling houses in San Diego, Masterson was stuffing election ballot boxes in Denver and Doc Holliday was dead. Front Street in Dodge City was a

★ Did Miles and Rosina Hutchinson consider alighting, or even ending their journey, at the settlement of Hutchinson on the banks of the Arkansas River in Kansas? They did not do so, but if they had they would have entered a burgeoning village of 8,000 mostly white inhabitants – many of them Amish – who made a living chiefly from agriculture and who were unable to buy a drink. Although Clinton Carter Hutchinson had since moved on to establish another town in North Carolina, his teetotal principles remained and Hutchinson was also known as Temperance City.

sleepier thoroughfare. The Long Branch Saloon and the China Doll brothel had recently closed. The Wickedest Town in the West was already living only on the remnants of its cattle trade, on its legends, its living memories and the echoes – as loud as yesterday – of the percussion of a long-barrelled Buntline Special.

At La Junta their train forked south-west through Trinidad and other nominal reminders of the fact that if they had taken this journey 40 years earlier they would have been passing through Mexico. Beyond Santa Fe they turned due west. In a moonscape of eerie chemical colours they stopped for the last time before journey's end at Navajo Springs, where a traveller in 1853 had noted with transparent relief that 'the water was gushing out of the ground in several places, but instead of the various runnels uniting into a brook, they overflowed the nearest low ground and transferred into a marsh, in the small pools of which, however, we found abundance of excellent water for ourselves . . .'

And then their carriage rumbled past low bluffs and mesas, past complex mud pueblo buildings from whose yards full-skirted Navajo women with their babies strapped to fixed wooden frames calmly watched them go. They saw shocks of corn. They rolled past occasional ramshackle cabins close to the track and ragged white men wiping the sweat from their brow. They slowed to walking pace as they chugged into a sparsely wooded basin in the desert. They saw a cluster of enough simple shacks to house four or five hundred people. They saw a shop, a couple of saloons, a single-storey main street – and with a final screech of brakes their train pulled to a halt at Holbrook station.

No precise statistical record of this place survives for the years before 1900. Holbrook did not feature in the 1880 Federal USA census for the excellent reason that the town did not then exist. It was not given its name until 1881, when the Atlantic Pacific railroad company decided to honour its chief engineer Henry Randolph Holbrook by calling its new little station in the desert after him. And the 1890 census records for almost the whole of the United States of America, including Holbrook in Apache County, Arizona, were destroyed in 1921 by a fire in the Commerce Building in Washington DC.

But there are clues to what the Hutchinsons and Wilkinsons found there in 1888. Other small European settlements similar to Holbrook existed in Arizona in the 1880s. One of them, Upper Gila, was also in Apache County. There, adjacent to the Mexican community of Lower Gila, a few dozen families scraped a living from the land. With the exceptions of a 55-year-old English carpenter and his Scottish wife, the adults were all in their 30s or younger. None but their infants had been born in the territory. They came from Illinois, New Zealand, Missouri, Pennsylvania, New York, Great Britain, Vermont and Texas. Those young people were, almost to a man and woman, farmers, labourers and homekeepers. They were not gunslingers or Indian fighters – they left that job to the soldiers at Fort Apache. They were not saloon keepers or bar-room whores. They had no church, as Holbrook had at first no church, no sheriff or civic administration. They had only their patch of cheap land, their few animals, their hardware store, their youth and their hope. They had their difficult but often uneventful lives in the fabled west; less idyllic than they may have expected, less precarious than later generations would imagine.

Holbrook was surrounded by a substantial, settled Navajo community. By 1900 some Native Americans were included in the United States federal census and the register of that year shows that 'mingled with the white population, residing in white families, engaged as servants or laborers, or living in huts or wigwams' within the precincts of Holbrook in Apache County, Arizona, there were 157 'Indians'. They composed almost exactly a quarter of the total population of Holbrook, which was 612. But we know that in 1880, for instance, from an estimated total 'Indian' population in the United States of more than 300,000, only 66,407 were included in the national census. As Arizona contained, after California, more Native Americans by far than any other territory or state in the union, and as the

Arizona natives at that time were more likely than most others to be 'not taxed' and 'roaming individually, or in bands, over unsettled tracts of country', those 157 registered tribesmen were – as residents of any ethnic origin would be fully aware – absurdly unrepresentative of the demographic balance of Navajo County.

We do not know exactly what the 157 Native Americans did in the vicinity of Holbrook. The census recorded their names – Slim Legs, Yellow Iron, Pas Lit So Ge, Son of Left Hand – and the fact that they had been locally born, but little else.

But we know that they were largely Navajo, an enormous and inclusive tribe of the Athabaskan language family which reached from the north-western territories of Canada to California, New York State, Utah and northern Mexico. Semi-nomadic, lodging in cabins of wood and clay known as hogans, they were often (although not universally – the militant Apache were a branch of the Navajo clan) tolerant of the white incursors despite their fraught experience of Europeans.

The Navajo had also over the centuries reached an accommodation with the Pueblo people, such as Hopi and Zuni, who had previously established themselves in the Great American Desert. By the nineteenth century they were growing maize and corn, breeding domesticated animals and erecting pueblos of their own. They wove uniquely beautiful rugs and blankets. They developed their own use for Arizona's mineral reserves; their silversmiths created bracelets, necklaces, earrings and the hand-clasps of hunting bows; their personal decorations included such semi-precious stones as turquoise, quartz and amethyst . . .

Given the numbers of Native Americans in the territory, given their pride and their mistreatment by the agents and representatives of Atlantic culture, it is mildly surprising that the few hundred people of Holbrook were not in the late nineteenth century swept from the face of the earth, let alone that Miles, Rosina, William and Elizabeth Hutchinson and Tom and Kate Wilkinson were in 1888 permitted to join them.

As early as 1680 the Navajo had allied with the Pueblo people to deter the Spanish conquest. In the 1840s they refused to accept

the legitimacy of the United States annexation of their homelands in Alta California and Santa Fé de Nuevo México. Punitive
actions against them by the US Army and freebooting militias
culminated in 1863 and 1864 when the Scots-Irish frontiersman
Colonel Christopher 'Kit' Carson raised havoc in the Navajo
lands, killing their livestock, incinerating their homes and crops,
and finally sending 8,000 men, women and children who had
surrendered with a guarantee of immunity on a 300-mile death
march through the desert before they were finally corralled onto
reservation lands which – with substantial boundary changes and
greater and lesser degrees of independence – would remain their
reduced and restricted homelands into the twenty-first century.

There were skirmishes and land-raids throughout the 1870s
and 1880s – including one bitterly ominous dispute featuring
several hundred armed and aggrieved Navajo in 1887, the year
before the Hutchinsons' arrival. But under the leadership of the
resistance-leader-turned-statesman Ashkii Diyinii, or Manuelito,
the majority of Navajo people had by then begun their long walk
to compromise with the remorseless power of the white United
States.

So when the young journalist Enoch Conklin was sent by the
Continent Stereoscopic Company of New York into the Great
American Desert in 1877, with the remit to produce a market-
able multi-media presentation of 'Picturesque Arizona', the
'Indians' were the least of his troubles.

Conklin saw what the Hutchinsons saw. He observed the
multi-racial character of the new colonial railroad townships:

> . . . an Indian village exists contiguous to it, and a full representa-
> tion of the old . . . tribes constitute an equal half of its daily
> population. Blanketed and half-nude Indians associate as inti-
> mately with the whites (what few there are here) as do the
> Mexicans themselves . . .
>
> One sees a mass of one-story buildings, built of adobe, and
> roofed with mud, the floors of which were originally the ground,
> but which have been, by the more thrifty foreigners of all classes

recently arrived, replaced by board ones. Some are whitewashed, and present a cleanly appearance; while others are the embodiment of the filth of the greaser . . .

The hour of eight, every morning now, when the train comes in, is an interesting one . . . There is then congregated, with eager eyes, Indians, Chinese, Americans; Jew, Gentile, and Pagan. In fact, most every nation and condition of men on the earth, one might be inclined to say, is represented. The same conglomeration, characteristic of all embryo places of the West, is here seen . . .

At night the Indian huts and camp fires may be seen glimmering around the city.★ As one approaches these and sees, crouched together, a handful of half-clothed, beggarly Indians, a feeling of sadness steals over him. They will sit with stoic stillness and stare at you with an awe-stricken expression as if they knew that their hour for final extermination was at hand. The fires perhaps, may be fading into dying embers. Upon this you will look and muse. For how typical, in its fading, is it of the very race to which it has given warmth and life. You count one, two, three, four, five remaining embers in the heap. There are just five Indians in the group. As quickly as those embers, must these Indians fade away under our civilization; and we wonder, that if, in our civilized state, were we truly so, this would be the case.

In the north-eastern corner of the territory, where the Hutchinsons and Wilkinsons were seeking another new beginning, Enoch Conklin noted with respect and a little surprise the settled agrarian society of the Arizona Native Americans which was 'fading away under our civilization'. But despite the civilising influence of the Pueblo people and their neighbours, Arizona could be a lawless place. Enoch Conklin's stagecoach was

★ 'It seems like a cruel pollution of the English language,' Conklin wrote elsewhere, 'to call these squatting places, cities, but when you are "among the Romans you must do as the Romans do." '

ambushed at night in the desert – but not by 'Indians', and not in a hail of arrows and bullets.

> I sat on the left of the driver. To the left of the horses' heads and facing us, stood a goodly specimen of physical man with a large revolver levelled at our heads. It was about the size, I should judge, of those used by the 'Horse Marines'. To the left of the stage, on a range with me, was another 'six-footer' with a hat, which, had it been mid-day, I would suppose was used to keep the sun off him, spreading out on all sides, and slouched down over his face. He held in his hands, and levelled at my breast a rifle.
>
> . . . And then, breaking the silence, came the demand for 'your money, or your life!' and the voices of these men seemed to echo from mountain to mountain.
>
> I was ordered to get down from the coach and stand before them; while the soldier inside was ordered 'to the front' to hold the horses' heads. Being a soldier, and one of his essential duties being to 'obey!' he was constrained, in his good judgment, to do so. Nobly did he perform his duty in this instance. Now, I had never been a soldier; yet, I obeyed orders in this case quite as well as he did. However, it was perhaps the stern force of "duty" that actuated him to obey, whereas mine was by force of persuasion. A rifle at your head and a six-shooter at your breast are terrible persuaders . . .
>
> Having secured my money, and evidently taking it for granted that the driver and the soldier had none (or being now satisfied with what they had obtained) we were told to resume our places on the coach. Having done so, the fire-arms being kept steadily upon us the while, we were ordered to drive off; and as we did so, the two men cried out alternately, 'Good-night!' 'Good-night!'

Just as not all Native Americans were violently opposed to white colonialism, not all whites were highwaymen. The few hundred people that the Hutchinsons and Wilkinsons joined in Holbrook in the late 1880s were engaged in a variety of respectable

European occupations. They were telegraph operators and druggists, school teachers and liverymen, barbers, shop-keepers and railroad agents. Unlike their Navajo, Zuni and Hopi neighbours, almost none of them had been born in Arizona. They came from Germany, Canada, California, Connecticut, New Jersey and a dozen other established states of the union. Like the people of Upper Gila and like the Hutchinsons and Wilkinsons themselves, they were young; the great majority being in their 20s and 30s. This was no country for old men.

Regardless of their different vocations, those few hundred whites were all in Holbrook for one reason alone: its railroad station. The railroad which had opened seven years earlier had not only facilitated their own arrival; it made possible the exports to the east and west from which the whites of Holbrook and the whole of Apache County could make a living.

There were several such exports. Miles Hutchinson and Tom Wilkinson pinned their hopes on one which had been identified ten years earlier by Enoch Conklin . . .

Just as not all of the desert is a waste of sand, so is not all of it fit for agriculture. Rocks and mountains here assert themselves in about the same proportion that they do in other countries. But these are far from valueless; this fact is being daily demonstrated as men begin to realize that the desert offers something worth looking for. Quartz-mills and smelting furnaces have already been erected on the desert mines of Ivanpah, Resting Springs and elsewhere on its western edge. Silver, lead and copper occur there in ores rich enough to excite the wonder of miners. Asbestos of remarkably long fibre is found near the San Gorgonio Pass. Gold occurs on its eastern edge in quantities great enough to have caused the celebrated Colorado River excitement of 1861; and mines of it are still worked at Chimney Peak and Carga Muchacho. Lead, silver and copper also occur as abundantly on this side, as on the western side of the desert.

These facts give credibility to reports of rich discoveries in mid-desert, made by prospectors too poor to develop mines at a distance from natural waters . . . Gypsum is a common product of the desert, widely diffused; flakes of selenite are found in nearly all the canyons coming in from the West, while great masses of this lovely mineral are found at many points. Pumice-stone of excellent quality is found on the railroad and in many other places; thousands of tons of it lie piled in masses; the engineers are now using it for polishing their locomotives . . .

Conklin had failed to notice or to mention the fossilised trees.

They lay scattered whimsically on the landscape around Holbrook like the collapsed and broken columns of a thousand Roman temples. Logs so perfect in their petrified preservation that from a distance of a few feet away they appeared to be recently fallen trees, some intact, some of whose bark had peeled off. Protected by the deep, dry earth for tens of millions of years, they had re-emerged into sunlight long before humans of any ethnicity entered the painted desert, and as the rough skin of Arizona and New Mexico was eroded by wind and occasional rain the logs continued to break through the topsoil; a literally unfathomable resource; mute representatives of prehistory.

The Pueblo people, the Navajo and Hopi knew of the treasure at the centre of those stone trees. Europeans were slow to catch up. Credit for their 'discovery' is usually given to the United States Army officer Lieutenant Lorenzo Sitgreaves of the Topographical Engineers Corps. In 1851, three years after the United States had absorbed Arizona into its territory, Sitgreaves was commissioned by the Senate to lead an explorative expedition into its extensive newfoundlands.

He and his 30-man escort rode westward from New Mexico up the Zuni River, past the cornfields, peach orchards and gardens of onions, beans and chile cultivated by the 'aborigines'. They met the Little Colorado River and on the fourth day of their journey, 28 September 1851, to avoid the riverbank which had been made muddy by recent rain Sitgreaves and his party made for higher ground in eastern Arizona. There, in a desert 5,600 feet above sea-level, they discovered that 'the ground was strewed with pebbles of agate, jasper and chalcedony, and masses of what appeared to have been stumps of trees petrified into jasper, beautifully striped with bright shades of red (the predominating colour), blue, white and yellow.'

The surgeon and naturalist to Sitgreaves' expedition, Dr Samuel Washington Woodhouse, satisfied himself in his own report by stating that on 28 September 'we passed the remains of a large petrified tree, the wood of which was agatised. It was broken in pieces, as if by a fall, and its root was up-hill. It must have been upwards of three feet in diameter.'

Two years later, in 1853, Lieutenant Amiel Weekes Whipple was despatched by Washington to survey a possible railway route from Memphis, Tennessee, through the new territories to the small town of Los Angeles on the Pacific shore. Whipple was tantalised to encounter 'Quite a forest of petrified trees . . . They are converted into beautiful specimens of variegated jasper . . . Fragments are strewn over the surface for miles.' Whipple took with him the German adventurer and artist Heinrich Balduin Möllhausen, who duly made a lithograph – the first visual depiction ever made by Europeans – of 'The Petrified Forest in the Valley of the Rio Seco'.

Despite such reports the resource remained largely unexploited by white Americans for a further three decades. In 1879 Lieutenant John Hegewald was sent to Arizona to collect samples of the phenomena for the Smithsonian Institution, one of whose executive regents, General William Tecumsah Sherman, had earlier spotted the stone trees of Arizona while traversing the territory. Hegewald was despatched with twelve men and two mule-wagons to collect '2 logs, say from 20 to 25 inches diameter and 6 or 8 feet long, weighing near a ton each' which Sherman envisaged 'would stand on end, in either side of the [Smithsonian] Museum'.★ In 1879, Hegewald reported:

★ They still do stand on end, in a corner of the Early Life hall of the Smithsonian's National Museum of Natural History in Washington DC.

I rode down the valley to examine the thousands of specimens that lay scattered on each side of the valley along the slopes, which were perhaps 50 feet high; the valley of the Lithodendron,⋆ at its widest part, being scarcely a half mile. Along the slopes no vegetation whatever was to be seen, wood being very scarce; the soil was composed of clay and sand mostly, and these petrifactions, broken into millions of pieces, lay scattered all down these slopes. Some of the large fossil trees were well preserved, though the action of heat and cold had broken most of them in sections from 2 to 20 feet long, and some of these must have been immense trees; measuring the exposed parts of several they varied from 150 to 200 feet in length, and from 2 to 4 feet in diameter, the centers often containing most beautiful quartz crystals.

When his men began winching two enormous specimens onto the wagons, Hegewald said that the curious local Navajo (who were herding 'thousands of head of sheep') 'thought it strange the "Great Father in Washington" should want some of the bones of the "great giant" their forefathers had killed when taking possession of the country.' The red lava deposits in the district were in Navajo mythology, Hegewald said, 'the remains of the blood' that ran from the giant's wounds.†

Petrified trees were not unknown in the United States. Individual specimens in California and Colorado also attracted national attention in the 1870s. But nowhere did forests of fossilised wood exist in such profusion as in the Arizona territory – and yet, despite the marketable value of such quartzes as chalcedony, agate and jasper, until the 1880s few civilians ventured into eastern Arizona to pick them like spring flowers off the desert floor.

⋆ Before the term Petrified Forest finally stuck in the twentieth century, the district was variously known as the Lithodendron (literally: stone trees) Valley and the Chalcedony Park.
† The Southern Paiute people of Arizona disagreed with the Navajo. According to another (white) Smithsonian ethnologist, they believed that the petrified logs were spent arrow shafts sent by their thunder god, Shinauav.

That was partly because until 1881 no railway line ran through the region. It was also because, despite the peaceable and even accommodating nature of most of the area's myriad nationalities of native people, some substantial tribes offered vigorous resistance to the white invasion. They included, as we have seen, the Navajo. They also included those cousins of the Navajo who came to be known as Apache.

The various Apache peoples, who probably arrived in what would become the south-western United States in around 1000 CE, had been resisting the Spanish occupation since the sixteenth century. In 1835 the newly independent state of Mexico placed a bounty on Apache scalps. There was an uneasy settlement with the North Americans after the Mexican–American war of the late 1840s, which was broken when US soldiers were deployed to protect white gold-diggers in Arizona. For 30 years thereafter the 'Apache Wars' were fought to the death. When that death came, it was the death of Apache culture, but until it came large areas of Arizona were risky territory for small bands of white men in search of semi-precious stones.

Despite the hostilities, it would be wrong to suggest that all contact between whites and Apaches between the 1840s and 1880s resulted in bloodshed. Enoch Conklin also spent a day with the Chokonen-Chiricahua Apache resistance leader Cochise three years before the latter's death at the age of about 59 in 1874. Conklin wrote,

He gave me a history of his wrongs, and although he had been the cause of killing more white men, than any other chief or Indian, and had been cruel beyond description in his tortures, I could not help but feel that he had been deeply wronged; and, that from the light given him, and the law and morals upon which he had been educated, he had acted conscientiously, and had done what he believed to be right. He was a man of great energy, of superior ability and firmness of purpose, and was generally faithful to his promises. He was tall, straight and commanding in appearance, and his features were regular with a placid, though rather sad countenance. He rarely ever smiled, and was thoughtful and studied in all his expressions. I talked to him of the superior advantages of civilization, but he replied, 'I am too old to adopt new customs.' He had captives with him who could speak and read the Spanish language, and he was well advised of everything the newspapers said about him. He expressed a desire that his children should learn to read and write, 'but of us old people', he said; 'you can make nothing of us but wild men'.

The last surrender, and the effective end of militant native resistance in the south-western United States, occurred in the town of Holbrook itself just two years before the arrival there of the Hutchinsons and Wilkinsons. The Chiricahua Apache warrior Goyaalé (the Yawner), who had been nicknamed Geronimo by the Mexicans after the ferocity of one of his assaults had caused their soldiers to plead in unison for the help of St Jerome, took up arms in his early 20s in 1851 after his wife, mother and three children were massacred in his absence by a company of 400 Mexican soldiers.

Over the next 35 years he became one of the most brilliant guerrilla military leaders in history. He fought the Mexican and United States armies simultaneously on both sides of the Rio Grande (whose recently acquired function as an aquatic border between two imperialist powers he naturally refused to recognise).

By 1885, with almost all of the other south-western tribes conquered, ethnically cleansed or subdued, Geronimo's band was reduced to 36 men, women and children roaming the highlands of Arizona and northern Mexico. Those three dozen people evaded 5,000 United States troops (almost a quarter of the entire US Army) and several units of the Mexican military for a year. In the autumn of 1886 Geronimo decided to surrender on his own terms. He considered that he would win better treatment from the Americans than the Mexicans (correctly, as it transpired – athough he was never allowed to return home, Geronimo lived until 1909, when he died at the age of 79 as an

Oklahoman farmer and minor celebrity), so he and his tiny band travelled to Skeleton Canyon in south-eastern Arizona and there he offered his truce to General Nelson Miles.

They were escorted north to the small new town of Holbrook. There, disarmed, they sat on the ground and waited by the five-year-old railroad station until a train arrived to carry them 2,000 miles east to Florida.

It was finally safe for Europeans to take the road to the riches of the Petrified Forest in Apache County in the United States territory of Arizona. Their only serious enemies would now be other Europeans.

Although I now know that I do not carry a single strand of Miles Hutchinson's DNA (mine is, it turns out, that of the waster George Hall, which all things considered makes much more sense), I do bear his name. I was christened Roger Miles Hutchinson, in direct tribute to my father's grandfather.

But while Rosina comes quite easily to me, I have to work at characterising Miles. Assemble all of the many details which we have about his life, put them into a coarse sieve, shake it thoroughly, and there is no dross. You are left only with nuggets of brave and honourable behaviour. Like most products of the old British working class, I am not given to idealising it, and Miles Hutchinson sits uneasily in a twenty-first-century mind. The nagging, almost irritating suspicion persists that what we now see is the straightforward paragon that Rosina got.

He was what once would have been called a simple man. That implies no intellectual deficiency, just that he devoted himself to his family and his work. Unlike his wife, Miles was illiterate. The only hobby for which he is remembered is sword-dancing. That gave rise after his death to a rumour that in his extraordinarily itinerant younger years he must have spent some time in Scotland. But there is no evidence that he ever went north of Hadrian's Wall, and he did not have to cross the border to learn sword-dancing. Throughout the nineteenth and into the twentieth centuries, sword-dancing was enormously popular in the Tyne and Wear pit villages. Select colliery teams of five male dancers would perform for money, and in tournaments, before large crowds in Newcastle, Sunderland and Durham.

It seems that Miles Hutchinson belonged to such a team. So we know that as well as being strong (he was a coal-face hewer), handsome, courageous and decent, he was also athletic, fast, agile and co-ordinated.

I have two photographs of Miles. The first was taken at some time in the 1910s, possibly to celebrate his sixtieth year in 1915 or 1916. It is a posed family group of Miles and Rosina and their eight surviving children. The four young men (including William, who was by then in his 30s and married with children of his own) stand behind the patriarch and matriarch. The two older girls sit on wicker seats at opposite ends of the group.

Miles is sitting quite erect, with his back as ramrod straight as a colonel of the horseguards. He is wearing a dark suit, waistcoat, collar and tie. His hair and moustache have been trimmed and combed (and he still has more of the former than does William, whose different genes are already causing him to bald dramatically at the temples). His face is thin, his cheekbones are pronounced and his eyes are deep-set. His unsmiling gaze is as uncompromising as his posture. His large hands are resting on his thighs. His youngest daughter is at his feet, and her left arm is draped comfortably, familiarly, gracefully over her father's knee.

The second photograph was taken some years later. It also is posed, but in an entirely different manner and for quite different reasons.

Miles Hutchinson is now older, in his late 60s, perhaps, or even his 70s. He is standing in his working clothes at the entrance to a pit shaft. His mining lamp hangs from his left hand and his right hand grasps a stout walking stick.

I cannot imagine why this photograph should have been taken and kept within the family, unless it was perhaps to mark his final shift, his last day down the mine. The fact that he permitted it is another reflection of a certain character, because even allowing for his age it does not show Miles Hutchinson at his Sunday best. His old working breeches, waistcoat and shirt are worn, grimy and stained. Instead of a neatly folded tie he is wearing around his neck his pitman's knotted scarf. His top-coat hangs baggily from his elderly shoulders; its collars are curling and frayed. His metal pit token, or check badge, which identified him as being at work, is pinned to his left lapel, weighing down the thin material at that side of the jacket. The ensemble is topped off by a large flat cap.

But his posture, despite the stick, is as proud as ever. His expression, despite the advanced years, is identically uncompromising. If you did not know better, you would describe his eyes as fierce.

Simple men devoted themselves to home and work. Those two photographs are how Miles Hutchinson preferred to be remembered. The first, the family group, is unexceptional. The second, at the mouth of the pit shaft, is extraordinary. He paused, stood still in his working clothes, wearing and carrying the emblems of his mining life, looked firmly at the camera lens and permitted someone to click the shutter. His permission was also his blessing – you would not have caught Miles Hutchinson unawares, or imposed upon him. No son, daughter or workmate could have taken that photograph without his consent. This is me, he allowed. Here I am, with everything including my principles intact, still standing.

The Petrified Forest

Arizona, 1888

John Bergson had the Old-World belief that land, in itself, is desirable. But this land was an enigma. It was like a horse that no one knows how to break to harness, that runs wild and kicks things to pieces. He had an idea that no one understood how to farm it properly, and this he often discussed with Alexandra. Their neighbors, certainly, knew even less about farming than he did. Many of them had never worked on a farm until they took up their homesteads. They had been HANDWERKERS at home; tailors, locksmiths, joiners, cigar-makers, etc. Bergson himself had worked in a shipyard.

— *Willa Cather,* O Pioneers! *(1913)*

In 1888 Miles Hutchinson and Tom Wilkinson built a cabin and a winter store. They will have erected it by the railroad line within walking distance of the modest centre of Holbrook. It was not a log cabin. Living – as opposed to calcified – trees were rare in north-eastern Arizona. In those latitudes, even at 5,000 feet above sea-level, thick layered planks were trusted to keep out the cold.

Then they went to work.

There were several ways of exploiting the resources of the Petrified Forest, and none of them involved quite the same level of danger or discomfort of deep-seam coal mining. Initially the most obvious and common method was to harvest the forest's rich crop of quartzes, its amethysts, chalcedonies, agates and jaspers, and its 'false topaz', citrine. A large but finite quantity of such stones was lying on the ground. When that supply had been exhausted the quartz miners were obliged to seek out the mother-lode, which was clustered in the middle of the 200-million-year-old fossilised trees. The logs were usually too hard to smash with an axe or a hammer, so the extraction process required explosives. As a report from the legislative assembly of Arizona Territory to the United States Congress eight years later, in 1896, would phrase it, the 'ruthless' miners 'are destroying these huge trees and logs by blasting them in pieces in search of crystals, which are found in the center of many of them . . .'

There was also, it was soon discovered, a market for the left-over blasted tree trunks once the quartzes had been removed and exported to the cities east or west along the Atlantic Pacific Railroad. That same Arizona legislature report told Congress that 'carloads of the limbs and smaller pieces are being shipped away to be ground up for various purposes'. Those 'various purposes' included making emery board and paper for polishing metals and smoothing ladies' fingernails. Once pulverised into grit, petrified trees made an excellent abrasive. This fact did not escape the Armstrong Abrasive Company of Denver. After a few years of buying chunks of stone wood from Arizona miners and transporting them north to be processed, the Armstrong Company built its own factory by the railroad in the Petrified Forest 17 miles east of Holbrook. The factory never opened. Just in time to prevent every fossilised tree in Arizona being ground into sand, a Canadian enterprise slashed the price of emery to a level which made Armstrong's Arizona operation unprofitable.

That setback did not much damage the living being made by men such as Miles Hutchinson, Tom Wilkinson and scores of other miners from Europe and the other American states. It was quickly realised that the biggest market for fossilised logs was in the fossilised logs themselves, polished, occasionally intact, but more often sliced into household ornaments and even building material.

This was not new. The ethnologist Walter Hough, who visited Arizona in the 1890s, recorded that:

In the celebrated Petrified Forest, which is some 18 miles from Holbrook, Arizona, on the picturesque Santa Fe Railroad, there are ruins of several ancient Indian villages. These villages are small, in some cases having merely a few houses, but what gives them a peculiar interest is that they were built of logs of beautiful fossil wood . . .

The prehistoric dwellers of the land selected cylinders of uniform size, which were seemingly determined by the carrying strength of a man. It is probable that prehistoric builders never chose more beautiful stones for the construction of their habitations than the trunks of the trees which flourished ages before man appeared on the earth. This wood agate also furnished material for stone hammers, arrowheads, and knives, which are often found in ruins hundreds of miles from the forest.

The White Eyes who arrived in force out of the east in the nineteenth century rarely if ever built whole dwellings from the logs. But they recognised their domestic possibilities. The process probably began in California, where a small number of fossilised redwoods had been found at Calistoga Springs. In 1871 it was reported from there that 'slabs of the [petrified] fir-trees are said to make beautiful mantels'.

In 1885 a Russian dealer made one Apache County miner's fortune by paying $500 for a round of petrified log 28 inches in diameter and 30 inches thick, which the Russian then proceeded to slice up into tabletops. The broken, fallen trees were also sold for inlay, panelling, floor tiles, mosaics and jewellery.

For the next two decades the produce of the Petrified Forest, although it made no local miner a millionaire, was in a seller's market. Cleaned, scoured and polished, stone wood was beautiful, unique, almost indestructible and became immensely fashionable. Samples of it were exhibited – along with the miraculous Actina device for curing blindness and deafness – at the World's Fair in Chicago. It was displayed at the Paris Exposition. The French sculptor Auguste Rodin was reported to be 'incredulous at the possibility' of a block of petrified tree. In 1885 Frédéric Bartholdi, the designer of the Statue of Liberty Enlightening the World whose constituent pieces had just arrived in New York harbour from France, was given from public subscription a $1,000 gold and silver statuette on a base of Petrified Forest agate.

Following a visit to Arizona in 1899 Lester Ward, a palaeontologist with the United States Geological Survey, wrote with barely restrained despair of the predation by commercial exploitation of what he considered to be a unique and irreplaceable American resource:

> Many years ago, the firm of Drake & Co, of Sioux Falls, undertook the work of manufacturing table tops, mantels, clock cases, pedestals, paper weights, and other articles of furniture and decoration out of these sections of agatized wood, by polishing the smooth surfaces and cutting them into the desired forms.
>
> I understand that Tiffany & Co, of New York, obtained through this company the beautiful pieces used by them for such purposes. I visited their house at the time they were engaged in this work, and through the courtesy of Mr George F. Kunz was shown some of the raw material that they then had in hand, consisting of several sections of immense trunks, of the most brilliant colors.
>
> While in the park the present season my teamster informed me that he was employed for a long time hauling these trunks out of the upper forest to Carrizo station. Although, according to all accounts, many carloads of it were shipped to the East, he said that there was a larger quantity left at the station that was not shipped than all that was removed at that time. As scarcely any of this remains at the station now, I asked him what had become of it, and he said it had been carried off little by little by anybody that wanted a piece.

The full extent of mining by hungry Europeans of the stone logs
and quartzes of the Petrified Forest during the last two decades
of the nineteenth century can never properly be gauged. But it
was clearly substantial. Those men put in a lot of hours. In 1903
an anonymous correspondent to the *New York Times* lamented
that:

> The petrified forest – the largest and most marvelous of its kind
> in all the world – in Northeastern Arizona has been woefully
> hacked to pieces and carted away wholesalely by vandal
> hands . . .
>
> Tons of petrified wood are still carted away from the Govern-
> ment lands, and during the past Summer five of the finest
> specimens of standing trees disappeared by piecemeal in one-
> and two-foot sections. But this is nothing to the manner of
> the destruction of the forests from the time the Santa Fe
> Railroad built through the region of the petrified forest in
> 1885 [sic] until two years ago [the writer meant to say between
> 1881 and 1901].
>
> A company of Colorado men engaged in the work of gather-
> ing carload lots of sections of the fossilized trees and in polishing
> slabs sawed from them. The petrifactions are as hard as flint and as
> beautifully colored as agate or onyx, and there are mantels, hotel
> bars, parlor tables and even wainscoting in the Middle West made
> from the priceless relics of unfathomable ages in the petrified
> forest . . .

Such reports and pressure from other sources led in 1906 to a
large but not complete section of Arizona's Petrified Forest being
designated a protected National Monument. While tourists were
still permitted to take away pocketfuls of quartz and fossilised
woodchips from within the prescribed region, wholesale commercial extraction was forbidden. But in the late 1880s all of that
was 20 years in the unimaginable future. Miles and Tom and
their colleagues could scour the desert for loose quartz, blast apart
fossilised trunks, haul specimens of logs to the railroad halts at

Adamana, Corrizo or Holbrook and sell them on to the agents of the Armstrong Abrasive Company, Drake and Co, Tiffany's and whoever else wanted to add a bit of market value to a piece of prehistory. In that respect at least, it was not substantially different from digging for coal. It goes without saying that they no more saw themselves as vandals than did they all come from Colorado. They were working men trying to claw a living from an essentially foreign land.

William Hutchinson was taught to read and write, add up and subtract chiefly by his mother. The small school in Holbrook which had been established in 1885 was open for ten months in the year and staffed at first by a succession of single schoolmistresses. A boy named John Fish (whose father and mother had moved west from Illinois and New York) who attended the Holbrook school in the 1890s remembered it as,

> . . . an old adobe one-room on the south side of the tracks . . .
>   One of the first school teachers that I can remember was a lady that was a very sweet old woman. I don't remember her name but Holbrook was too much for her, so she didn't stay very long . . . The school board hired a man by the name of Mr Young, a well-qualified man for the job. When he came in, I can remember he had a bull-whip and a six-shooter that he laid at the other side of his desk. He said, 'I have been hired to handle the school in place of a woman who couldn't handle the bullies, so I don't want any trouble out of any of you . . .'

But attendance was sporadic. Many pupils, especially boys, avoided the old adobe one-room and Mr Young's bull-whip. 'I would say to my sisters, you go on, I'll stay here,' recalled another student of the time. '. . . my mother didn't know. I'd stay all day long under a bush, maybe go fishing, all by myself. And I'd wait for the girls to come back and then go home with them . . .' In the late 1880s, when young William Hutchinson was in the district, only 27 of the local children were registered. The recently established *Holbrook Times* would comment that a dog fight in the schoolyard on any Saturday afternoon would attract more than twice as many children as were to be found in the classroom between Monday and Friday.

When not attending or dodging school, William could help his father search for semi-precious stones, some of which he was allowed to sell himself to the increasing number of sightseers arriving on the Atlantic Pacific railroad. 'We made a little purse,' said his contemporary, John Fish, 'and put a strap around our necks and displayed our various pieces of petrified wood and the passengers would come out and say, "How much for your petrified wood?" We would answer and tell them whatever we could get, or thought we could get, judging by the way they were dressed, and that was the way we earned our spending money.'

Such Tom Sawyerisms aside, it was an exhilarating boyhood for William Hutchinson. He was in an enchanted landscape. Beyond his family's and their neighbours' cabins, beyond the rough gardens, beyond dry arroyos and the multi-coloured plain rose low buttes and mesas. An apparently empty tundra was in fact, when subjected to the intimate inspection of a child, littered with objects and phenomena of boundless curiosity. As well as the miracle of the sparkling stone logs, low round hills striped with all the different pastel shades of a candy bar rolled off into the distance. 'Away on the horizon,' wrote the nineteenth-century Boston journalist and author Lilian Whiting after getting off the Atlantic Pacific train at a halt in the middle of the Petrified Forest and looking north, 'gleamed an evanescent, palpitating region of shimmering color. Yet this was not the "quarry of jewels" but the "Bad Lands", which have at least one redeeming virtue, whatever their vices – that of producing the most aerial and fairylike color effects imaginable.'

The bad lands were unsuitable places for cattle and sheep and were cordially hated by their herders, but by the late 1880s they were safe enough playgrounds for a boy of six or seven. William Hutchinson was more likely to encounter a camel on the high plateau than a dangerous wild animal or a hostile human being.*

As the sun set he saw, in the contemporary words of Lilian Whiting, 'a panorama of kaleidoscopic wonder. Afar to the horizon the Bad Lands shimmered in a faint dream of colors under the full moon. The stars seemed to hang midway in the air, and frequent meteors blazed through the vast, mysterious space.' When the sun rose again he would clamber over collapsed ancient walls. He could scrape from the earth strange skeletons, beads, rings and necklaces.

He was surrounded by the vestiges of a pre-European culture. On the boulders and gargantuan slabs of stone that littered the low mesa cliff faces were strange antique designs which could intrigue a boy for hours. They were already officially recognised as petroglyphs, but most whites in 1880s Arizona would know them simply as Indian rock carvings. Over millennia the sand-stone and basalt of the high plateau had acquired a 'desert varnish', a hard, dark skin of iron or manganese, bacteria and other organic deposits which when chipped away revealed the lighter colour of the rock beneath. This provided a natural canvas for a form of etching: a readymade plate for the creation of mezzo-tint in the wilderness. Before and after the arrival of Europeans on the American continent, in pre- and post-Columban times, people had, using hammer-stones and chisels, perfected this artistic process. They left behind – for precise reasons which

---

* Camels had been imported from Egypt into the Great American Desert by US Army personnel 30 years earlier, in 1856. They were abandoned when the Civil War in the 1860s called the south-western military units back east, and were still to be seen roaming wild in the 1880s. A boy of William Hutchinson's age called Douglas MacArthur, whose father commanded a garrison in New Mexico and who would himself have a formidable military career in the next century, was startled in 1885 when 'One day a curious and frightening animal with a blobbish head, long and curving neck, and shambling legs, moseyed around the garrison . . . the animal was one of the old army camels.'

disappeared with their civilisations★ – astonishing outdoor murals of male and female human figures, heads and masks; cougars, birds, lizards, snakes, bats, coyotes, horses and rabbits; bear paws, bird tracks, cloven hooves and human feet or handprints; textile and pottery designs, spirals, circles and other geometric shapes.

They were still, in the 1880s, everywhere and unignorable. Within a few short years, by the early 1890s, many of those historic relics would be plundered, like the fossilised trees, for profit. In 1903 one witness wrote:

> In that vast arid region designated as the Great American Desert covering as it does almost the entire Territories of Arizona and New Mexico . . . are to be found thousands of examples of simply wonderful handiwork of primitive communal peoples . . .
>
> For a dozen years the Southwest has become a touring point annually for thousands of visitors . . . These peripatetic visitors have created a tremendous demand for the art products of the ancient freeholders.
>
> In consequence a new industry has sprung up and every town vaunts its curio and bric-a-brac shop, where a conglomeration of minerals, rare and otherwise; modern Indian paraphernalia made to order, brand-new basketry and pottery, and often scores and scores of fine examples of art from the sites of ancient buried cities or from the former nestlike homes of the cliff peoples are to be found. Even the solitary trader at the water tank [where the Atlantic Pacific steam locomotives stopped for as long as it took to refill] has become afflicted with the bric-a-brac epidemic and peddles his pre-historic wares through the halted train, to the

★ Twentieth- and 21st-century (white) ethnologists have driven themselves half-mad in search of an original, logical 'function' of the petroglyphs of the American south-west. Semi-convincing arguments have been advanced in favour of their use as solar calendars. Lay observers of the clever, whimsical and apparently random carvings may however be tempted to dismiss logic, function and practicality and consider instead the perennial human yearning for mere artistic expression.

edification of the passengers and usually to the proprietor's financial satisfaction.

The discovery of the commercial value of such specimens has given rise to keen competition among the traders over this entire region, and the fact that several large collections have sold for fancy sums has so stimulated their cupidity that mercenary collectors have entirely outstripped scientific men in the search for and the acquisition of these articles and have committed the most pernicious acts of vandalism.

As petroglyphs were usually attached to slabs of rock weighing several tons, they will not have made their way easily into the tray of the trader at the water tank, or the retail items of small boys at Holbrook station. But they were often fragmented by nature and by humans. The 1,000-year-old treasure trove of the Great American Desert would not see out the nineteenth century intact.

While their husbands were hacking a living out of the hard earth and their son and nephew was footloose in Wonderland, Rosina Hutchinson and Kate Wilkinson had a household to run, an infant girl to raise, another new daughter to bring safely into the world and a rough frontier settlement to negotiate.

Rosina had given birth to another girl, a sister to young Elizabeth and William. For reasons which, once again, will be explained, we do not know her name. We can only guess, and Catherine would be as good a guess as any, in honour of her indomitable sightless aunt.

To describe such a place – and there were many such places – as Holbrook in the 1880s as an impossible town in which to raise a young family with peace and plenty and security would be contrary to the evidence of history. If that had truly been the case, if Holbrook and its equivalents were incapable in the 1880s and 1890s of supporting normal human life, if lawlessness and violence had been impossibly commonplace, then too few ordinary young families would have stayed there to see the town into the twentieth century.

But they did. John Fish's teacher who left because 'Holbrook was too much for her' was the exception rather than the rule. Most of her neighbours and fellow immigrants not only stayed, they also grew in number – and to a surprising degree, they thrived. Holbrook was described in 1883 as 'a wild and woolly town with a population of about two hundred and fifty persons'. The fact that the 1890 census was lost prevents us from knowing exactly what its white population was seven years later, but in 1900 it was 450. That was not a huge increase. But by all circumstantial accounts the town had grown rapidly in the 1880s and contained at the time of a great civic tragedy in 1888 perhaps a thousand people or more. Then fate struck little Holbrook and its population – a population which in 1888 included the Hutchinson and Wilkinson family – shrank as quickly as it had grown. It would be the middle of the twentieth century before Holbrook rose again to be more than what one resident called 'a wide place in the road'.

The illuminative point about Holbrook's early history in the 1880s and 1890s is not that it was small but that it did not disappear altogether, like so many other Arizona ghost towns. The railroad which had established the place continued to feed it, supplying new blood, the dependable delivery of freight and opportunities for trade. 'Holbrook,' writes the Arizona journalist and Apache historian Jo Baeza, 'was the center of a trading area with a hundred-mile radius. The railroad brought feed and supplies for the Navajo Reservation, the Mormon settlers and homesteaders, and the army at Fort Apache. Wool, hides and cattle were shipped out . . .'

The town which in 1888 Rosina Hutchinson and Kate Wilkinson called home had in 1881 – just months after the railroad opened – a general store named the Arizona Cooperative Mercantile Institute (which also hosted a branch office of the Wells Fargo 'overland mail' delivery service), and had opened its first post office in 1882. In the single year of 1883 no fewer than 25 new businesses started up in Holbrook. Santiago Baca located a liquor and general store on what would become the main street. Mrs A.M. Boyer opened the Apache Hotel – 'Everything the Best; New, Neat and Clean'. The German twins Adolph and Ben Shuster ran another general store. There was Field & Harvey's Grocery, Perkins & Spiers Cottage Saloon, Lindenberger's Bakery, Mrs Frank's Millinery and Dressmaking, Dr Robinson's Pharmacy, Boyer & Trimble's Carpentry & Builders', Breed Bros Store and William Wilson's Blacksmith and Wheelwright Shop. There was a gunsmith, a jeweller, a meat market, two hotels, two billiard parlours, a livery stable, a surveyor's office, a Chinese laundry and a Chinese cafe owned by Louey Ghuey. There was Adamson & Burbage's General Store, whose 'gentlemanly clerk' Will Yancey would be acclaimed as 'the most deservedly popular salesman in Holbrook'.

It was as though, on top of their railroad import/export activities, every one of the few hundred adult white people in Holbrook had invented in their desert oasis a functional closed economy and were fully engaged in selling things to one other. In 1884 the village even had a newspaper, the *Holbrook Times*, which felt able in its first issue to assert that 'Holbrook has a future that is unmistakeably bright. It is a radiating center for stockmen, ranchmen and miners . . . At present our town is well supplied with enterprising men.'

Another Englishman, Henry Scorse, who had been born the son of a poor agricultural labourer in Somerset in 1851, had emigrated to the United States at the age of 18, had made his way slowly south-west and wound up at the age of 30 in Apache County. There in 1881 he immediately met and married a spectacularly beautiful 17-year-old Hispanic girl called Julianita Garcia, and the couple proceeded to produce and raise in Holbrook a child every two years for the next two decades. By the time the Hutchinsons and Wilkinsons arrived in 1888 Harry Scorse owned to the north of the town a ranch of 10,000 head of cattle, sheep and horses which had suffered in but survived the last Apache wars. He had opened the Pioneer Saloon and would adjoin it with H.H. Scorse's Dry Goods, Groceries and Hardware Store.

Holbrook's facilities and opportunities in the late 1880s contrasted favourably with those of Billy Row or any other mining village in County Durham. Miles and Tom could work hard for the certainty of a reasonable income and the possibility of a windfall. Rosina and Kate could shop and mingle with a small but determinedly civilised society of other white women.

There was one defining, crucial difference. The dark and violent side of Holbrook manifested only occasionally, but when it did show its face, for a few hours or days the violence was so wild-eyed and furious that it obliterated the Arizona sun. It left most of the merchants, milliners, miners and hoteliers of Holbrook shocked and shuddering. It left some of them wondering about their future.

Dane Coolidge, the New Yorker who became an early-twentieth-century romancer of the American West, would claim from his new home in California 50 years later that in the 1880s there had been 26 deaths 'by the gun route' in Holbrook between one January and the next. Even though deaths 'by the gun route' were more likely to involve self-inflicted wounds and the manslaughter of colleagues through accidental discharge than deliberate homicide by cold-eyed sharpshooters, Coolidge, who was a prolific sensational novelist before he turned his hand to history, was exaggerating. Twenty-six premature deaths would almost have decimated its population (and reduced by a quarter its adult male population) year after year until nothing was left of Holbrook but a few traumatised widows and the Navajo families in the shadows at the edge of town.

But white men – almost always men – did occasionally shoot and kill one another in the Great American Desert. If there ever was an antebellum period of fabled innocence and peace in the vicinity of Holbrook, it was the few short years between the town's foundation in 1881 and the arrival of the Hashknife outfit just five years later.

The Hashknife – a crescent-shaped single-handled blade, similar to the French *hachoir* and the Italian *mezzaluna* (half-moon), used by chuck wagon cooks – was the brand of the Aztec Land and Cattle Company. In February 1886 the consortium of eastern businessmen and Texan ranchers who owned that enterprise bought from the Atlantic and Pacific Railroad company a huge swathe of Arizona. The Aztec paid the Atlantic Pacific the colossal sum of $500,000 for a range which ran fragmentarily up to 40 miles each side of the railroad for 650 miles west of the New Mexico border. Aztec topped up its investment to over $1,000,000 through the purchase of cattle, horses and equipment.

Before the end of 1887 the Aztec Land and Cattle Company shipped up to 40,000 head of longhorn cattle, 2,000 horses and several hundred cowboys onto its new range by rail from Texas, disembarking them piecemeal off the cattle trucks as the train made its halting way westward across Arizona.

Cattle were not new to Apache County. But this unprecedented quantity of grazing beasts put an impossible strain on the local ecology and on the human relations of northern Arizona. The ecology would crack within 13 years. Land which could support at best – in its virginal prime – only two or three beasts on every square mile was quickly overgrazed by a herd which grew, as the Aztec Land and Cattle Company strove to recover its million dollars, to 60,000 head.

Then came the droughts. Then came the floods. A Mormon settler would recall:

> When we came to Arizona in 1876, the hills and plains were covered with high grass and the country was not cut up with ravines and gullies as it is now. This has been brought about through overstocking the ranges. On the Little Colorado we could cut hay for miles and miles in every direction. The Aztec Cattle Company brought tens of thousands of cattle into the country, claimed every other section, overstocked the range and fed out all the grass. Then the water, not being held back, followed the cattletrails and cut the country up. Later tens of thousands of cattle died because of drought and lack of feed and disease. The river banks were covered with dead carcasses.

William Benjamin Cross settled in 1886 as a teenager with his abandoned Norwegian mother a dozen miles outside Holbrook.★ He recounted how,

> The famous Hash Knife cattle company shipped in and unloaded 60,000 cattle in the Holbrook district with the result that in the next two years they not only ate all the grass but trampled the roots until there was no grass left.
>
> The cattle would travel miles each way from the river looking for feed, and would come to the river to get filled up on water. The trail from the table lands to the water was long and steep. The cattle were so thirsty they would take a few steps in the water and stand and drink until they were bogged down and couldn't turn around to get out. The result was that hundreds died standing in the water and mud.
>
> The men working down the river knew if there was one, there was hundreds of dead cattle in the river three miles above, and all the water they had to drink was off the dead cattle.

A blizzard and two feet of lying snow in the winter of 1898/1899 finished off what was left of the Aztec Cattle Company's Arizona ranch. In 1900 the company liquidated its holdings in the territory.

Human relationships had buckled long before. Different accounts survive of the nature of the Hashknife cowboys who swarmed in and around Holbrook from 1886 onwards. Joseph Petersen, a citizen at the time of St Joseph, a Mormon settlement ten miles west of Holbrook, said:

> Most of the Hashknife cowboys I knew were good men, like [the wagon bosses] Frank Wallace and Barney Stiles. The outlaws just

★ Louisa Gulbransen's husband, a veteran of the Union Army in the Civil War named David Cross, had simply disappeared into the North American continent one day in 1885, never to be seen or heard from again. The following year Louisa decamped with her son William and three other children from their home in Illinois, caught the cross-country train to Holbrook and joined a small group of her Mormon co-religionists in Arizona.

followed the outfit from Texas. A former Hashknife cowboy, the tall, stooped Uncle Dick Grigsby (of whom it was said that 'the whiskey finally killed him, when he was ninety-seven'), would protest that 'Hashknife men weren't mean like a lot of people said. There were a few hot-headed kids, but most were good cowboys.

There certainly must have been a majority of hardworking herdsmen in the boys – boys who carried such names as Billy St Joe, Loco Tom Lucky, Ace of Diamonds, Poker Bill and Johnny-Come-Lately – who followed the Hashknife cattle from Texas to Arizona. And as the Aztec Company recruited locally it found itself almost obliged to draw on a labour force of Hispanics and Navajo, the latter in particular being excellent horsemen. Photographs of cowboys in north-eastern Arizona in the late nineteenth and early twentieth centuries prove at least one counter-intuitive fact: in many cases and many places in the old west, there was no conflict whatsoever between cowboys and Indians. There could not possibly be such conflicts: they were often the same people. Despite what was written in the novels of Dane Coolidge, the cowboys were the Indians and Indians were the cowboys.

However the Navajo cowboys entertained themselves during their leisure time, those of European origin liked to go into Holbrook and get 'a haircut' – drunk. The combination of alcohol and firearms was occasionally fatal (shooting incidents which resulted in the death or injury of white men, even in the 'wild and woolly' territory of Arizona, were often reported in the local and the east-coast newspapers, and it can be no coincidence that an overwhelming majority of them took place in and around saloons). Shortly after the first appearance of the Hashknife crew in Apache County in 1886 four men were drinking and playing cards in Perkins' Cottage Saloon by the railroad track in Holbrook. Three of the men were employees of the Aztec Cattle Company. An argument erupted, guns were drawn and fired. Two white men escaped west on borrowed horses; two Mexican cowboys were left dead on the ground. A passer-by remarked that Perkins' Cottage Saloon looked as if a bucket of blood had been spilled on the floor. Perkins' Cottage Saloon was instantly renamed the Bucket of Blood Saloon, to the advantage of local legend and the distaste of the Holbrook bourgeoisie.

In the following year, 1887, a young man named James Henry Walker arrived in Holbrook from Massachusetts. It would later be recalled that Walker was short and stocky and wearing yellow patent leather shoes, that he walked into the Frontier Saloon, flashed a thick billfold, bought drinks all round and informed the appreciative Hashknife crew that he, James Henry Walker, lately of Massachusetts, wished to become a cowboy.

Walker was naturally humoured by the Hashknife boys, who kitted him out in tight striped pants, shiny black high-heeled boots and spurs, a red silk shirt, a ten-gallon hat and 'a pair of silver-mounted, white-handled .45 six-shooters with a full cartridge belt'. They christened their creation the Cimarron Kid. Walker had probably noted the word 'cimarron' on a number of wild south-western topographical features and was happy to accept the monicker, without ever learning that in Mexican Spanish it was most commonly used to describe a feral sheep.

It hardly mattered: James Henry Walker would not live sober enough for long enough to care. Over the following weeks, the last weeks of his life, he got drunker and drunker and became involved with some of the Hashknife crew in a series of increasingly violent stunts. Walker progressed from being arrested for shooting out some lights and windows to being arrested on suspicion of shooting dead two cowboys. Released on parole from the Holbrook lock-up, he proceeded to get drunker than ever one Saturday night at Tom Pickett's White Saloon. In the early hours of Sunday morning Walker infuriated Pickett by repeatedly hammering one of his silver-mounted, white-handled .45 six-shooters on the bar of the White Saloon and demanding another drink. It was the apotheosis of the Cimarron Kid. Pickett asked Walker if he wanted to shoot it

out. Walker agreed. The two men squared up. Pickett told
Walker to shoot first. Walker did shoot first, and missed Pickett
by three clear feet. Pickett then took his time over shooting the
drunk dead. The Hashknife crew used the $6,000 found in his
belongings to buy themselves a lot of whiskey and to buy James
Henry Walker a coffin and a funeral service.★

In a small town – a village, a hamlet – such ferocious and
percussive outbursts of bloodletting, however infrequent, were
deeply disturbing. But individual cowboys, even fantasy cowboys, were an annoyance to the rest of respectable Holbrook
without much affecting the citizens' daily lives. By definition,
cowboys spent most of their time out on the range, not in the
settlements. The Hashknife crew would turn up in the town's
saloons when passing by, or on an occasional break, or while
assembling cattle outside town to await the arrival of stock cars
on the railtrack. They would often be asked to hand in their
weapons and to leave Holbrook that very night, after a Chinese
meal or a steak, several whiskeys and a spell in a Front Street
'pleasure parlour'. Even when still armed cowboys did tend to
kill or injure only other cowboys.

The rustlers and the range wars which arrived in the cowboys'
wake were at a different level of concern. They fretted constantly
at the fringes of the wider settled community.

Just as some cowboys were Indians and Indians were cowboys,
so rustlers were also cowboys and some cowboys were also
rustlers. Where there were cattle herds there were cattle rustlers.
There had been both cattle and rustlers in Arizona before the
arrival of the Aztec Company, but not on such a scale. Several of
the Hashknife crew moonlighted – multi-tasked – from the
other side of the range. Jo Baeza writes:

★ Even in the frontier territories – perhaps especially in the territories – some
semblance of the rule of law had to be seen to be applied. The deputy sheriff
who had arrested and then released James Walker got a coroner's jury out of
bed on that very same Sunday morning. The jury, which by then would have
come to regard James Henry Walker as an entirely uninvited nuisance, instantly
ruled that Tom Pickett had acted in self-defence.

Some Hash Knife men got their start in the cow business with company calves. Most of the men 'had something' on each other and could blackmail their friends into keeping quiet. Some were reluctant to turn in their range pals. For that reason – and the fact that the owners were in New York – stealing was easy. Tom South, a Hash Knife cook, stole a bunch of Aztec cattle and drove them to Colorado, where he sold them and bought a saloon with the money. When the saloon went broke, Tom South returned to Arizona and went back to work with the Hash Knife.

If rustling from the Aztec Company had been a strictly inter-necine affair, if company cowboys had stolen only company cattle, other, smaller local ranchers such as the Englishman Henry Scorse may have remained unperturbed. But of course it was not so constrained. Ranchers already established in northern Arizona resented the Aztec Company's appropriation and over-exploita-tion of such a vast amount of land, and its high-handed disregard for their modest interests. On top of that, the Aztec Company was followed from Texas into Arizona by a number of freelance, independent cattle thieves who were not at all choosy about whose beasts they rustled. 'Thousands of longhorns ate the grass,' said one Arizonan settler, 'riffraff and hell-hounds out of Texas ate the ranchers' beef.' Some small ranchers retaliated by rustling the Aztec Company's cattle themselves. Some Aztec Company hands responded by pistol-whipping small ranchers.

Into this stew of grievance and resentment was added the fact that much of northern Arizona had previously also been sheep country. Weight for weight, sheep require roughly as much grazing land as do cattle. A range war was therefore almost inevitable. What became known as the Pleasant Valley War would rage for almost ten years from the late 1880s to the late 1890s. It was boiling when the Hutchinsons arrived and it would still be simmering when they left.

The Aztec Company was not formally involved in the Pleasant Valley War. But it seems certain that the squeeze put on small established herdsmen by the Aztec's massive incursion into Arizona caused the friction which created the spark. The Pleasant Valley War was a feud between two families, one with an interest in sheep and the other with an interest in cattle. Its first fatality was a Navajo shepherd employed by the Tewksburys, who was ambushed and shot dead on a disputed grazing in February 1887 by a member of the cattle-rearing Graham clan. It reached its blood meridien the following year when one of the Graham faction named Andy Cooper was heard in a Holbrook saloon bragging that he had ambushed and killed two Tewksburys.

The extraordinary personality of Commodore Perry Owens then entered the fray. Owens had been born on a Tennessee farm in 1852. At the age of 13 he ran off to Oklahoma and then New Mexico. By 1881 he found himself working in Arizona as a ranch foreman. Perry Owens had grown into a hard, quiet and practical man who was also an extremely accurate shot. In 1886 he was elected sheriff of the whole of Apache County. Perry Owens had no intellectual pretensions whatsoever, but he was something of a dandy. He wore his straight blond hair very long, either coiled up inside his stetson or flowing down over his shoulders to his breast-bone. He wore a generous walrus moustache, goat-hide chaps and a cartridge-belt.

When Andy Cooper left the saloon that afternoon Perry Owens followed him to the home in Holbrook of the Blevins family, another chapter of the Graham party. The sheriff could not have known, although he might have guessed, that there were three men, three women and six children in that small house when he approached it carrying his cleaned and loaded Winchester. He knocked on the door. Cooper answered it. Owens saluted and said that he had a warrant and wanted Cooper to 'come along with me'. Cooper demurred, so Owens took a step back and with his Winchester repeating rifle shot his suspect in the stomach. John Blevins, who had a young wife and a baby boy in the building, fired a gun from behind an interior door, missed Owens and hit a horse. Owens then shot John in the shoulder.

Owens walked back into the street and fired off a shot at the house. A man called Moses Roberts jumped from an upstairs window with a gun in his hand. Owens shot him. The 16-year-old Sam Houston Blevins grabbed the dying Andy Cooper's gun and – with his screaming mother in pursuit – charged out of the front door. Owens shot the teenager dead.★

Commodore/Sheriff Perry Owens then strolled the short distance back to the livery stable. According to the *Holbrook Times*, 'several citizens went to the house, where a horrible sight met their gaze. Dead and wounded in every room, and blood all over the floors, doors and walls.'

Once again a coroner's jury was assembled. It was called by Perry Owens in his dual role as elected sheriff and county coroner, and it found that Sheriff Owens had been 'entirely justified' in his actions. A granddaughter of the survivor John Blevins, Ruth Blevins Chesney, would later write that respectable Holbrook was angry with its new sheriff for causing such bloodshed in the middle of town, and for killing two men – young Sam Blevins and Moses Roberts – for whom he had no arrest warrant.

Holbrook's response to the massacre was ambiguous. The town would certainly have preferred its county sheriff to kill people in the open countryside – there was, after all, plenty of it. But where bad men like Andy Cooper were concerned, Holbrook may have been prepared to be open-minded about the technicalities of arrest warrants. The verdict of its coroner's jury of several adult white male registered voters indicates as much.

But the Blevinses were what passed in young Holbrook for an established family, even if they might be keeping poor company and involving themselves in an unfortunate feud. A year later in 1888 John Blevins, injured shoulder and all, was sentenced for his part in the affray to a term in Yuma Territorial Prison. A petition

★ Only one of the four casualties lived. Sam Blevins died on the spot, Andy Cooper died the following day and Moses Roberts died a few days after that. John Blevins survived, with a shoulder injury and a grudge, both of which would affect him for the rest of his life.

was raised in Holbrook requesting that John Blevins – who was by then almost the only male adult Blevins left alive in the Pleasant Valley War – be pardoned. Enough influential local names were appended to the petition to convince Governor Conrad Zulick (an east-coast liberal who had been parachuted into the Arizona governorship from New Jersey in 1885) to grant the pardon. John Blevins returned to his vocation as a stockman and proceeded to raise in Holbrook a large, handsome and respectable family, although he never again talked to Commodore Perry Owens.

The Hutchinsons and Wilkinsons arrived in the district in the year that John Blevins was pardoned. They can have been there for little more than a month or two, absorbing the settlement's idiosyncratic blend of dissolution and respectability, gentility and violence, hospitality and hostility, comfortable routine and panic attacks, when Holbrook was burned almost to the ground.

The fire began an hour before noon one midsummer Saturday in 1888 – the time of the day of the week when women from around the area would be trawling through the Holbrook shops, men would be meeting in the saloons and their children would be playing with friends in the street. In the 80–90 degree Fahrenheit dry heat of a Holbrook June it did not take long for the flames from Henry Scorse's wooden warehouse, which was packed to the rafters with wool, to spread. The nearby Holbrook House Hotel was quickly consumed. No resident died but an eye-witness reported in the *St John's Herald* that 'the inmates had barely time to get out of the burning buildings with their lives, losing all of their personal effects. Several traveling gentlemen stopping at the Holbrook Hotel lost their trunks filled with samples and two of them lost their coats and other apparel'.

Then Schreiner's Bakery went, then Schuster's Store. The Apache House Hotel turned to ashes, followed by Dr Robinson's Pharmacy, Krohn's Shoe Shop, Rehfeld's Barber Shop, Adamson and Burbage's Store, Lindenberger's Bakery, A.M. Boyer's Lodging House, the Atlantic and Pacific Railroad Depot, three ice houses, two feed corrals and many private homes. 'A scene of wild confusion was visible at every turn,' reported the *St John's Herald*. 'People carrying household goods into the street, then in less than ten minutes were obliged to carry them to another place for safety and on returning with another armful find those already carried out to be in flames, and in the end all were destroyed in the fire-fiend.'

This Biblical *deus ex machina*★ culminated with the destruction of ten saloons.

It was said that Holbrook never properly regained its feet. Most of the buildings, especially the private houses, had been uninsured. Aid was sent from other parts of the region, and many of the business people and residents rebuilt with adobe and brick, but the small, short boom of Holbrook, Territory of Arizona, was cut off in its pomp. Fifteen years later, in 1903, the *Albuquerque Chronicle* would conclude that 'The fire was a blow from which Holbrook never fully recovered. Part of the town was rebuilt but not half of what burned. Where there were ten saloons before the fire, there is one now, and the same ratio may be applied to the amount of money and people to be found there, then and now.'

Although they may have contributed to their growing disillusion, neither rifle shots nor burning buildings drove the Hutchinson and Wilkinson families out of Arizona. They cannot have been comfortable, those four adult northern Europeans, in the fierce heat and the penetrating cold of Arizonan summer days and winter nights. They would surely have missed the comfort foods of their English upbringing. They would have been distressed by the fact that feuds and squabbles which at home would have been pursued with insults or fisticuffs, in America led to guns being drawn and fired and people being killed. The

★ The fire was not directly started by humans. It was not the result of arson or a casually thrown cigar-butt. It apparently began when the hot sun burned through a thick glass window in Scorse's warehouse and ignited the wool inside, much as a cowboy might light a camp fire through the prism of a magnifier.

women could have fretted at the immense distance which now lay between them and County Durham. The men could have seen the work of a miner in the Great American Desert for what it was: a wearing vocation which could barely support their families and which rarely if ever made a working man rich.

But their decision to leave was finally determined by death, and by the prospect of another new life.

In 1888 Rosina Hutchinson was pregnant once again. During her pregnancy her two baby daughters, the children whose names we have imagined to be Elizabeth and Catherine, both died.

They were not unique. It has been estimated that in the nineteenth-century United States infant mortality rates varied between 130 and 230 deaths in every 1,000 births. That is, as many as a quarter of all young children died of diarrhoea, respiratory illnesses and infectious diseases such as scarlet fever, measles, whooping cough, smallpox, diphtheria and croup. But we do not know, we cannot know which malignant toxin killed them. They died. There was no minister, vicar or priest in Holbrook, no church and no consecrated land. Elizabeth and Catherine Hutchinson could not be left to lie forever beside Andy Cooper and the Cimarron Kid in some frontier Boot Hill. So their graves were dug with dull resignation and simple dignity by Miles Hutchinson and Tom Wilkinson in the thin earth behind their cabin.

When next morning the sombre family began its day, Miles and Tom and Rosina and Kate and William discovered that during the night the two small bodies had been dug up and mutilated by jackals or other wild desert animals.

That was the last straw. Rosina would not give birth to another child in the Territory of Arizona. She began to pack. Her husband and her brother-in-law went outside again with picks and spades.

The surface of the Great American Desert was more rock than soil. But even after all that had passed they were still coalminers from the Tyne and Wear field, and they had never sunk a more valuable shaft. They cut deep into the desert floor, piling stones up beside the mouth of their tunnel. They hacked at the ground relentlessly. They reached a depth of six feet, of eight, of ten, one man relieving the other in regular shifts. They stopped when they could dig no more. They laid the swaddled remains of Elizabeth and Catherine in their warm, dark tomb at the bottom of the pit. They shovelled stones on top until the shaft was full again. They re-erected two small crosses. They built a sturdy timber fence around the grave. Rosina, Kate and William cast desert flowers on the small mound. Then they all went home.

A numismatist will already have spotted the flaw.

Remember the buffalo nickel? I turned to it again just now. As they were on the way home, so was the buffalo nickel, deep in a safe recess of my young grandfather's clothing.

But it did not come home with him. It could not have come home with him. It had not yet been coined. I discovered that in a celebrated online encyclopaedia. (Reluctant to believe it, I also treble-checked. Then I deca-checked.)

There are photographs online of both sides of my grandfather's nickels. It is the same coin, from the beard on the crouching buffalo to the two feathers hanging from the Indian's hair.

This is what the entry reads:

> *The Indian Head nickel, also known as the Buffalo nickel or Bison nickel, was an American nickel five-cent piece minted from 1913 to 1938. It was designed by sculptor James Earle Fraser . . .*
>
> *Fraser featured a profile of a Native American on the obverse of the coin, which was a composite portrait of three Native American chiefs: Iron Tail, Two Moons and John Big Tree. Big Tree claimed his profile was used to create that portion of the portrait from the top of the forehead to the upper lip. The 'buffalo' portrayed on the reverse was an American Bison, possibly Black Diamond, from the Central Park Zoo.*
>
> *Soon after the Indian Head nickel went into circulation, it became apparent that the reverse design was problematic; the 'FIVE CENTS' inscription, which was on a raised mound at the bottom of the reverse, was one of the highest spots on the coin, and thus wore away very quickly. As a result, the design was modified by Charles Barber during its first year of*

production. Barber removed the raised mound and lowered the relief of the inscription so that it would not wear away as quickly, along with other design changes. However, one problem that was not addressed was the placement of the date. Like 'FIVE CENTS' in the original design, the date was placed at a relief that exposed it to a great deal of wear . . .

This issue was never definitively addressed by the Mint, so many Indian Head nickels have their dates partially or completely obliterated through extensive circulation . . .

An interesting design variety was produced in 1937 (one year before the production of these nickels was stopped) – the 1937 '3-Legged' buffalo nickel. The buffalo's right foreleg is gone on this rare error. This was produced when the leg was accidentally ground off in the process of removing marks from the die. In uncirculated condition this coin is worth a significant amount of money. Some normal buffalo nickels have had the front leg ground down as an attempt to mimic the more valuable die error, but these can be distinguished by other features present on the '3-Legged' buffalo nickel.

Most buffalo nickels were removed from circulation in the 1950s and 1960s in various degrees of wear, although it wasn't uncommon with diligent searching to find one as late as the early 1980s. Today, any talk of a buffalo nickel showing up in circulation is notable, as approximately 1 in 25,000 nickels in circulation today is a buffalo nickel. Many of these have the date completely worn off.

It is then a coin with an outstanding history, which is more difficult to discover in twenty-first-century America than in my house in the Scottish Hebrides, where you can find a buffalo nickel any day of the week, but which suffered from one persistent and celebrated design flaw: the date wore off after it had been used to buy a soda pop and a couple of candy bars.

The only date which is ineradicable from the buffalo nickel is this one: it was first minted in 1913. It cannot therefore have found its way into my grandfather's pocket in the late 1880s.

But it was his. As neither he nor my father are around any more to explain the life story of his buffalo nickel, I must conjecture. And I suppose that at some time in the 1910s, 1920s or 1930s the buffalo nickel was posted as a keepsake to my grandfather by somebody in the United States . . . somebody he knew in the United States.

They came back, a surprisingly large number of them came back. But most of the emigrants stayed. They stayed at the bottom of graves, like his two younger sisters. They stayed in limbo, like his lost Aunt Rachel, neither dead nor alive but swallowed up in the vast, inscrutable continent.

Or they stayed as some of his uncles stayed, sinking mines in the western Pennsylvania coal patches, raising families there, growing old and American there, losing as the decades passed their north-eastern English accents and even some of their memories of home. But never quite forgetting the bright-eyed infant who grew into boyhood with them after that first walk west. One day, as an elderly man, Uncle Christopher found himself admiring the beautifully designed five-cent coin among his spare change and thought, Willie would like that . . . I wonder if Willie remembers . . .

THE KNOWN

10

Return Emigrants

County Durham, 1901

> We carried in the steerage nearly a hundred passengers: a little world of poverty . . . The history of every family we had on board was pretty much the same. After hoarding up, and borrowing, and begging, and selling everything to pay the passage, they had gone out to New York, expecting to find its streets paved with gold; and had found them paved with very hard and very real stones.
>
> *– Charles Dickens, American Notes* (1842)

They took the long train back to the Pittsburgh coal patch. There in 1889 Rosina gave birth to a son who was christened Thomas – clearly after Kate Wilkinson's husband, the man who had announced on his westward passage all those years ago that he was really a farmer by vocation and not a coalminer at all. Thomas Hutchinson might have first seen the light of day in the United States of America, but when his mother completed the census form in later years she would adamantly, protectively insist that young Tom's entry stated: 'Born USA – British Citizen'.

As soon as Rosina felt that baby Thomas Hutchinson was ready to travel they retraced their journey across the eastern continental divide to Philadelphia. And there, back on Delaware Wharves, they boarded a ship and steamed over the Atlantic Ocean to Liverpool.

It may have been a heavy-hearted homecoming. But if they wanted consolation, Rosina and Kate and Miles and Tom could have gained some from the realisation that they were very far from being the only emigrants to give up on the New World and return to the Old. The ships going home contained almost a third of the emigrants who had earlier crossed the Atlantic Ocean in a westerly direction.

They returned in their millions, for as many different reasons as they had left. And they returned in differing degrees. Some ethnic, religious, national or cultural groups went home again in great numbers, others barely went home at all. Hardly a single Amish man or woman, for instance, returned to Switzerland or Alsace from Pennsylvania or anywhere else in the New World.

Similarly, as little as 5 per cent of the Jewish peoples of Europe who crossed the Atlantic in the late nineteenth and early twentieth centuries ever went back to the *shtetl* to face discrimination, eviction, hatred, pogrom and later holocaust. The Irish who fled their own mid-nineteenth-century famine had nothing to return to but starvation, so an understandably small proportion of them ever saw Ireland again. And the large numbers of Irish men and women who made their new homes in Boston, Chicago, New York, New Orleans and elsewhere carved out such a substantial livelihood and sub-culture for themselves in America that they were able to offer hospitality and a degree of security to their compatriots who followed them, with the result that even many years later, even into the twentieth century, decades after the end of the Great Famine, no more than 10 or 11 per cent of Irishmen and women who emigrated to the USA ever went back to live permanently in Cork, Killarney or Dublin. Comparatively small numbers of Welsh and Scottish people left on the emigrant ships, but once in the United States between 80 and 90 per cent of them also tended to settle. They were usually (although not always) English-speakers after all, which gave them a linguistic pass onto the higher slopes of the US economy.

In the cases of the Welsh and the Scots, it can be difficult to distinguish in the statistics between those who emigrated with a new beginning in their hearts but then gave up and straggled home, and those who travelled to and from the United States only for a long holiday or to visit relatives, but never had any intention of settling there.

There is a similar dichotomy in the figures for workers from eastern and southern Europe. Large numbers of Greeks, Italians, Poles and Croats undoubtedly went to the USA to find work. Equally undoubtedly, large numbers of them – more than half – subsequently went back to Greece, Italy, Poland and Croatia. What is in doubt is how many of that 50 or 60 or (in the cases of the Serbs and Bulgarians) 90 per cent of migrant workers were driven from the USA back to Europe again by the financial and other exploitations to which an untrained, illiterate and incomprehensible peasant workforce was prone, and how many of them ever actually intended to resettle in the United States for good – how many of them, in short, only crossed the Atlantic to raise quick cash to improve their standing when (not if) they returned home to southern and eastern Europe.

As we saw in Pittsburgh, there had been within Europe a long tradition of migrant workforces travelling for seasonal work from the poor lands to the richer industrial or rural economies of France and Germany. Italians spent their summers harvesting grapes in Burgundy and grain in Provence; Swedes and Poles travelled in their tens of thousands to earn marks in the factories of Prussia. Very few of them ever had intended to stay in France or Germany. Their purpose was to take enough money home to support their families, or to improve the size of their family's holdings, or to establish themselves as prospective family men back in Italy, Sweden or Poland.

When steamships made the transatlantic crossing quick, cheap and dependable, many such Europeans simply substituted the USA for France or Germany or Italy. Millions of southern Italians travelled across the Atlantic in the 50 years of the Golden Age between 1870 and 1920. At least 60 per cent of them sooner or later went back to Italy.

Italians, especially from the bitter south, had few if any industrial skills and little English, could consequently not command great wages, and were often the subjects of racial and religious hostility within the USA. Their homelands were certainly poor, but they had not run away from genocidal famines or pogroms. They had something to return to, and the majority of them reached the opinion that they would sooner grow old and die in Italy than in Manhattan.

The English had all the advantages that the Italians lacked. They spoke English – they had invented the language. They were often literate. They usually possessed the skills necessary to a developing economy. They were generally white, Anglo-Saxon and Protestant.

But for all those silver tickets into North American prosperity, a fifth of all English emigrants returned home from the USA. Out of the two million men, women and English children who travelled to live in the United States, some 400,000 looked around and then went back again. They also had not fled famines or pogroms. They also had something to return to. And they decided that they would rather grow old in County Durham than in Pennsylvania.

Perhaps in the end it was not failing to find a cure for blindness, or failing to strike gold, or losing Rachel, or losing the two girls, or even an amalgam of all those disappointments and tragedies. Perhaps something more fundamental propelled them onto the ship going back to Liverpool at Delaware Wharves. Perhaps it was at heart nothing more or less than the lure of green fields and black pitheads, mild summers, north-country accents, reliable food, the laughter of family and old friends. They had been to see the elephant jump the fence – and it had jumped! Boy, had it jumped. It had jumped quite high enough for six lifetimes.

They never wandered again.

A decade later, in the spring of 1901, a national census enumerator was making his way efficiently along the doorsteps of the village of Ryton in County Durham on the south bank of the River Tyne. Ryton-on-Tyne was the village in which the businessman Angus Watson had been born 27 years earlier, and in which he had been raised. By 1901 Watson had left to pursue his career, and later write down his childhood memories of the lives of the villagers and colliers of those earlier times; but the old market cross still stood in Ryton, surrounded by the twelfth-century Norman church, the two venerable country inns, the Squire's Hall, the Manor House and the Home Farm with its 'hay-ricks, its clucking fowls, and flock of turkeys'.

Just a mile to the west of this bucolic scene, still within the parish of Ryton, the census enumerator walked with his forms and his pencils into 'a huddle of little houses built in rows'. He had entered the pit village of Addison Colliery. It was an expanding enterprise in 1901. Just five years earlier there had been just 240 miners employed by the Stella Coal Company at Addison. By 1901 there were almost 500 men working there underground.

The enumerator was told that three people lived at the terraced pit cottage No. 108 Addison Colliery in the spring of 1901. They were a 45-year-old man named Thomas Wilkinson, his 43-year-old wife Catherine, and Catherine's widowed mother, Elizabeth Robson, who had been born in Philadelphia, County Durham, 80 years earlier. Thomas was occupied as a coalminer. We do not know whether or not the enumerator was told – or guessed – that the childless Catherine was blind. There was no reason to put that information on a census form.

If there were no children in No. 108 Addison Colliery, next door made up for it. At No. 109, the adjacent building, lived the 45-year-old Miles Hutchinson and his 37-year-old wife Rosina. Miles was employed as a 'coalminer hewer'. There were also seven youngsters in the cottage. Eighteen-year-old William was employed as a 'coalminer putter'. His 12-year-old younger brother Thomas, nine-year-old John and seven-year-old Rosina were at school. Five-year-old Alice, two-year-old Miles and one-month-old Rachel were playing and crawling and being dandled around the two cottages, receiving – the enumerator might have noticed – considerable practised attention from the middle-aged Catherine and the elderly Elizabeth at No. 108.

William still did not know that Miles Hutchinson was not his genetic father, and that his six younger siblings were his half-brothers and half-sisters. On the morning of William's wedding three years later to a girl called Mary, Miles would take his adopted son to one side and tell him the truth about William Hall and Rosina and Miles himself. 'Well,' said William stoically, 'if it's all right with you, I've always been a Hutchinson and a Hutchinson I'll remain.'

But that was all still to come. In 1901 the census enumerator recorded in his careful copperplate the birth places of all the members of the household. Miles had been born in Swaledale in the county of Yorkshire. Rosina and all her children but one had been born in County Durham. The exception was 12-year-old Thomas. He had been born in America. But he was, Rosina Hutchinson insisted, a British citizen.

Perhaps at the end of the interview Rosina, with her one-month-old daughter Rachel in her arms, drew the enumerator's attention back again to Thomas. 'He's a British citizen, mind, wherever he was born. Mind that's on there – a British citizen.'

Notes

Chapter 1 Rest-stops on the Road

p. 12: 'There were "electro-vital forces" in the human physique, argued the qualified Chicagoan physician . . . which could be 'augmented or diminished at pleasure, by the application of artificial electricity.' *The Body Electric, How Strange Machines Built the Modern America*, Carolyn Thomas de la Pena.

p. 13: 'that no person shall practice electro-therapy . . . trained nurse.' *New York Times*, 13 April 1897.

p. 13: 'to compete with irregular electrotherapists . . . purchased by unlicensed practitioners.' *The Body Electric, How Strange Machines Built the Modern America*, Carolyn Thomas de la Pena.

p. 16: 'the British populace of the nineteenth century . . . overseas emigration.' 'Labour Mobility', Jason Long and Joseph Ferrie, *Oxford Encyclopaedia of Economic History*.

Chapter 2 Between the Sea and the Soil

p. 24: '. . . often consisted of a "but-and-ben" . . . hung like a pall over the village.' *My Life*, Angus Watson.

pp. 24–25: 'He [the collier] was generally a keen gardener . . . his neighbours.' *My Life*, Angus Watson.

p. 25: '. . . whom I began to admire and respect . . . and realise all that I learned from them.' *My Life*, Angus Watson.

Chapter 3 Tales of Ordinary Freedom

p. 38: 'to represent to the House . . . the House may think proper.' *Journal of the House of Commons*, vol. 85.

p. 39: 'We have no crown . . . but we never forget our native land.' *The Dalesmen of the Mississippi River*, David Morris.

Chapter 4 Sisters

p. 47 (footnote): 'This was not so unusual as later generations might have imagined . . . premarital sex. *Sexual, Marital and Family Relationship of the English Woman*, Eustace Chesser.

p. 51: 'beyond the Seas for the Term of Seven years.' Offences Against the Person Act (1828).

Chapter 5 Hell With the Lid Taken Off

pp. 63–64: 'Group after group of picturesque devotees . . . the surrounding people.' *A History of American Christianity*, Leonard Woolsey Bacon.

p. 64: 'the Amish, Old and New . . . communities prospered.' *Chronicles of America*, Yale University Press.

p. 64: 'the object of the grossest outrage . . . a movement to put a stop to the outrages.' *New York Times*, 26 June 1895.

p. 64: 'a plain, unpretentious sect of farmers who wear broad-brimmed hats and hooks and eyes on their clothes instead of buttons.' *New York Times*, 12 May 1888.

p. 65: 'by a party . . . the village band furnished music'. *New York Times*, 12 May 1888.

p. 68: 'the blackest, dirtiest, grimiest place in the United States.' *The WPA History of the Negro in Pittsburgh*, J. Ernest Wright.

p. 68: 'smoke, smoke, smoke – everywhere smoke . . . Hell with the lid taken off.' *Atlantic Monthly*, James Parton.

pp. 71–72: 'putrefied . . . they drank directly from Pittsburgh's polluted Monongahela and Allegheny rivers.' *Carnegie*, Peter Krass.

p. 72: 'Whiskey was considered medicinal . . . Christmas and the Fourth of July'.' *Carnegie*, Peter Krass.

p. 74: 'It is common for the mining camp . . . landlord and store-keeper as well.' *Patch/Work Voices, The Culture and Lore of a Mining People*, Dennis Brestensky, Evelyn Hovanec and Albert Skomra.

p. 75: 'The term "American miner" . . . so far as the western Pennsylvania field is concerned, is largely a misnomer.' United States Immigration Commission Report, 1911.

p. 77: 'Yes sir, I got clubbed often . . . He would come around and club you and call you a son-of-a-bitch and [say] "quicker, quicker" . . .' *Coalcracker Culture*, Harold W Aurand.

p. 77: 'foreman's authority . . . he presented them as suggestions.' *Coalcracker Culture*, Harold W. Aurand.

p. 78: 'Immigrants poured into the country . . . where the other brothers and sisters already worked.' The Speeches and Writings of Mother Jones', Edward M. Steel.

p. 79: 'poorly built . . . cold in the winter.' *Patch/Work Voices, The Culture and Lore of a Mining People*, Dennis Brestensky, Evelyn Hovanec and Albert Skomra.

pp. 79–80: 'The design of company houses . . . hydrants provided water.' *Coalcracker Culture*, Harold W. Aurand.

p. 80: 'The remarkable thing about those mine patches . . . made no difference what religion you were or anything.' *Patch/Work Voices, The Culture and Lore of a Mining People*, Dennis Brestensky, Evelyn Hovanec, and Albert Skomra.

p. 81: 'they spent a good deal of time . . . from the surrounding hills.' *A Daisy of a Town*, Mary Elaine Lozosky.

p. 82: 'It is a small steel vial . . . five dollars apiece.' 'The Great American Fraud', Samuel Hopkins Adams, *Collier's Magazine*, 1905.

p. 84: 'Actina . . . bad English.' 'The Great American Fraud', Samuel Hopkins Adams, *Collier's Magazine*, 1905.

p. 84: 'The Actina . . . twenty-five cents to make.' 'The Great American Fraud', Samuel Hopkins Adams, *Collier's Magazine*, 1905.

p. 86: 'scores of petty fakers who flit from city to city doing a little business in eye lotions . . . glass eye.' 'The Great American Fraud', Samuel Hopkins Adams, *Collier's Magazine*, 1905.

p. 87: 'a singularly agreeable and frank specimen of the genus Quack.' 'The Great American Fraud', Samuel Hopkins Adams, *Collier's Magazine*, 1905.

pp. 87–88: 'I find the trouble . . . after five months.' 'The Great American Fraud', Samuel Hopkins Adams, *Collier's Magazine*, 1905.

Chapter 6 The Irish Channel

pp. 97–98: 'The differences . . . between the two.' 'English and American Railways', *Harper's Monthly*, 1880.

p. 98: 'imposing splendor . . . New York fire-engine.' 'English and American Railways', *Harper's Monthly,* 1880.

p. 98: 'The Englishman . . . they are in England.' English and American Railways', *Harper's Monthly*, 1880.

pp. 99–100: 'well equipped . . . American smoker.' English and American Railways', *Harper's Monthly*, 1880.

p. 100: 'if all the passengers . . . more arbitrary.' 'English and American Railways', *Harper's Monthly,* 1880.

p. 100: 'In the rude railroading of the primitive South and West . . . [they are] invaluable.' English and American Railways', *Harper's Monthly* 1880.

p. 101: 'The only way . . . "skip the town"' *New York Times*, 16 March 1884.

p. 101: 'The drift . . . under the sun.' 'Virginia Characteristics', *New York Times*, 11 August, 1881.

pp. 101–2: 'In Richmond . . . without pavements.' 'Virginia Characteristics', *New York Times*, 11 August 1881.

p. 102: 'The motto of the State should be "Virginia for the Virginians", and the white Virginians at that . . .' 'Virginia Characteristics', *New York Times*, 11 August 1881.

p. 102: 'talked with . . . "nigger domination".' 'Virginia Characteristics', *New York Times*, 11 August 1881.

pp. 102–03: 'a young man . . . cruel and unjustifiable.' 'Virginia Characteristics', *New York Times*, 11 August 1881.

p. 103: 'We have allus been a-making tobacco yer . . . but now we air a manufacterin' it.' 'All Through Virginia', *New York Times*, 17 January 1887.

p. 103: 'new tobacco factories . . . ground out.' 'All Through Virginia', *New York Times*, 17 January 1887.

p. 103: 'it is not hard . . . white and black.' 'All Through Virginia', *New York Times*, 17 January 1887.

pp. 104–05: 'The uneven cobblestones . . . strange and delightful.' *Fabulous New Orleans*, Lyle Saxon.

pp. 105–06: 'In the balconies . . . was French.' 'New Orleans', Charles Dudley Warner, *Harper's New Monthly Magazine*, 1887.

p. 107: 'It is a driving place . . . literature.' *Life on the Mississippi*, Mark Twain.

pp. 107–8: 'We come to look upon New Orleans . . . like a Parisian.' 'New Orleans in Winter', *New York Times*, 16 March 1884.

p. 108: 'are mostly Germans . . . Irish or American.' 'New Orleans in Winter', *New York Times*, 16 March 1884.

pp. 110–11: 'The Irish . . . in the streets.' *Forgotten Doors*, M. Mark Stolarik.

p. 111: 'will watch the progress of this proposed legislation with great interest . . .' *New York Times*, 30 May 1886

p. 112: 'White mens up thisaway would jes' as soon kill a nigger as eat dinner!' *Fabulous New Orleans*, Lyle Saxon.

p. 113: 'An inch of vanilla . . . honey.' *A River of Whiskey*, Chris Morris.

pp. 115–16: 'Although it was . . . terminated all.' *The World As I Have Found It*, Mary L. Day Arms.

Chapter 7 Nothing Exists But Mind

p. 120: 'It is plain that God . . . divine Love.' *Science and Health With Key to The Scriptures*, Mary Baker Eddy.

p. 120: '[Eddy] has launched . . . Mrs. Eddy's waistbelt.' *Christian Science*, Mark Twain.

pp. 120–21: 'Christian Science . . . this statement.' *New York Times*, 29 May 1899.

p. 122: 'She was middle-aged . . . a smile.' *Christian Science*, Mark Twain.

p. 122: 'Within the last quarter of a century . . . patient's imagination.' *Christian Science*, Mark Twain.

p. 123: 'see daylight . . . he will be entirely cured.' *New York Times*, 26 February 1858.

p. 125: 'Three times . . . all waving their wings.' *New York Times*, 20 August 1888.

pp. 125–26: 'Why, brothers and sisters . . . I don't dance now.' *New York Times*, 20 August 1888.

Chapter 8 The Painted Desert

p. 131: 'the hotel keeper and his son . . . Making in all nine living beings.' *Picturesque Arizona*, Enoch Conklin.

p. 135: 'the water . . . for ourselves . . .' *The Refugee*, Balduin Mollhausen.

pp. 138–39: '. . . an Indian village . . . the case.' *Picturesque Arizona*, Enoch Conklin.

p. 140: 'I sat on the left . . . "Good-night!".' *Picturesque Arizona*, Enoch Conklin.

pp. 141–42: 'Just as not all . . . their locomotives.' *Picturesque Arizona*, Enoch Conklin.

pp. 142–43: 'the ground . . . white and yellow.' 'Report of an Expedition down the Zuni and Colorado Rivers', 1851, Captain Lorenzo Sitgreaves.

p. 143: 'Quite a forest . . . for miles.' Report of Pacific Railroad Survey, 1853, Lieutenant Amiel Weekes Whipple.

p. 143: 'would stand on end, in either side of the [Smithsonian] Museum.' 'The Object at Hand', Adele Conover, *Smithsonian Magazine*, June 1997.

p. 144: 'I rode . . . quartz crystals.'. 'The Object at Hand', Adele Conover, *Smithsonian Magazine*, June 1997.

p. 144: Hegewald said that the curious local Navajo (who were herding 'thousands of head of sheep') . . . that ran from the giant's wounds. 'The Object at Hand', Adele Conover, *Smithsonian Magazine*, June 1997.

pp. 145–46: 'He gave me a history . . . wild men". *Picturesque Arizona*, Enoch Conklin.

Chapter 9 *The Petrified Forest*

p. 153: 'In the celebrated Petrified Forest . . . the forest.' Smithsonian Institution Annual Report, 1899.

p. 153: 'slabs of the [petrified] fir-trees are said to make beautiful mantels.' *New York Times*, 1 January 1871.

p. 154: 'Many years ago . . . wanted a piece.' *Glimpses of the Cosmos*, Lester Ward.

p. 155: 'The petrified forest – the largest and most marvelous . . . petrified forest.' *New York Times*, 12 July, 1903.

p. 156: 'an old adobe . . . any of you.' *Holbrook Tribune-News*, centenary edition, 1981.

pp. 156–57: 'my mother didn't know . . . then go home with them.' *Holbrook Tribune-News*, centenary edition, 1981.

p. 157: 'We made a little purse . . . spending money.' *Holbrook Tribune-News*, centenary edition, 1981.

p. 157: 'Away on the horizon . . . effects imaginable.' *New York Times*, 22 July 1906.

p. 158: 'a panorama . . . mysterious space.' *New York Times*, 22 July 1906.

pp. 159–60: 'In that vast . . . acts of vandalism.' *New York Times*, 12 July 1903.

p. 161: 'Holbrook . . . cattle were shipped out.' *Holbrook Tribune-News*, centenary edition, 1981.

p. 162: There was Adamson & Burbage's General Store . . . 'the most deservedly popular salesman in Holbrook.' *Holbrook Tribune-News*, centenary edition, 1981.

p. 164: 'When we came . . . dead carcasses.' *Mormon Settlement in Arizona*, James H. McClintock.

p. 165: 'The famous Hash Knife . . . dead cattle.' *Holbrook Tribune-News*, centenary edition, 1981.

pp. 165–66: 'Most of the Hashknife . . . good cowboys.' *Holbrook Tribune-News*, centenary edition, 1981.

p. 167: 'a pair of silver-mounted . . . cartridge belt.' *Holbrook Tribune-News*, centenary edition, 1981.

p. 169: 'Some Hash Knife men . . . Hash Knife.' *Holbrook Tribune-News*, centenary edition, 1981.

p. 171: 'several citizens . . . doors and walls.' *Holbrook Tribune-News*, centenary edition, 1981.

p. 172: 'the inmates . . . other apparel.' *Holbrook and the Petrified Forest*, Catherine H. Ellis.

p. 173: 'The fire was . . . then and now.' *Holbrook Tribune-News*, centenary edition, 1981.

Chapter 10 Return Immigrants

p. 185: 'hay-ricks, its clucking fowls, and flock of turkeys.' *My Life*, Angus Watson.

p. 185: 'a huddle of little houses built in rows.' *My Life*, Angus Watson.

Bibliography

Printed Sources

Books

Arms, Mary L. Day, *The World As I Have Found It*, New York, 1878

Armstrong, Thomas, Adam Brunskill, London, 1952

Aurand, Harold W., *Coalcracker Culture*, Susquehanna, 2003

Bacon, Leonard Woolsey, *A History of American Christianity*, New York, 1897

Brestensky, Dennis F., Hovanec, Evelyn A. and Skomra, Albert N., *Patch/Work Voices, The Culture and Lore of a Mining People*, Pennsylvania, 1977

Brown, Dee, *The American West*, New York, 1995

Center City Philadelphia in the 19th Century, Library Company of Philadelphia, New Hampshire, 2006

Chesser, Eustace, *Sexual, Marital and Family Relationship of the English Woman*, London, 1956

Chronicles of America, Yale University Press, New Haven, 1921

Clark, Andrew and Nairn, George, *Durham Coal*, Durham, 2001

Conklin, Enoch, *Picturesque Arizona: Being the Result of Travels and Observations in Arizona During the Fall and Winter of 1877*, New York, 1878

Cooter, Roger, *When Paddy Met Geordie*, Sunderland, 2005

Davies, Norman, *The Isles*, London, 1999

de la Pena, Carolyn Thomas, *The Body Electric, How Strange Machines Built the Modern America*, New York, 2003

Eddy, Mary Baker, *Science and Health With Key to The Scriptures*, Massachusetts, 1875

Ellis, Catherine H., *Holbrook and the Petrified Forest*, San Francisco, 2007

Garvey, Joan B. and Widmer, Mary Lou, *Beautiful Crescent, A History of New Orleans*, New Orleans, 1982

Gill, Mike, *Swaledale, Its Mines and Smelt Mills*, Derbyshire, 2004

Holbrook, Stewart H. *The Golden Age of Quackery*, New York, 1959

Husson, Therese-Adele (author), Kudlick, Catherine J. and Weygand, Zina (eds) *Reflections: The Life and Writings of a Young Blind Woman in Post-Revolutionary France*, New York, 2002

Krass, Peter, *Carnegie*, New Jersey, 2002

Lorant, Stefan, *Pittsburgh, The Story of an American City*, Pittsburgh, 1964

Lozosky, Mary Elaine, *A Daisy of a Town*, Pennsylvania, 2003

Lozosky, Mary Elaine, *Daisies, Dignity and Daily Life*, Pennsylvania, 2004

McClintock, James H., *Mormon Settlement in Arizona*, Phoenix, 1921

McKinney, Louise, *New Orleans, A Cultural History*, New York, 2006

Miller, Randall M and Pencak, William (eds), *Pennsylvania, A History of the Commonwealth*, Pennsylvania, 2002

Mills, Alan, *Mining and Miners in 19th Century Swaledale and Arkengarth-dale*, Reeth, 2006

Mollhausen, Balduin, *The Refugee*, Leipzig, 1862

Morris, Chris, *A River of Whiskey*, Alberta, 2002

Morris, David, *The Dalesmen of the Mississippi River*, York, 1989

Saxon, Lyle, *Fabulous New Orleans*, New York, 1928

Steel, Edward M. (ed.), *The Speeches and Writings of Mother Jones*, Pittsburgh, 1988

Stolarik, M. Mark, *Forgotten Doors*, Washington, 1988

Trimble, Marshall, *Roadside History of Arizona*, Montana, 2004

Twain, Mark, *Christian Science*, New York, 1907

Twain, Mark, *Life on the Mississippi*, Boston, 1883

Varney, Philip, *Arizona Ghost Towns and Mining Camps*, Phoenix, 1994

Ward, Lester, *Glimpses of the Cosmos*, New York, 1913

Watson, Angus, *My Life*, London, 1937

Whipple, Lieutenant Amiel Weekes, Report of Pacific Railroad Survey, Washington, 1853

Wolf, Edwin, *Philadelphia, Portrait of an American City*, Philadelphia, 1990

Wright, J. Ernest, *The WPA History of the Negro in Pittsburgh*, Pittsburgh, 2004

Wyman, Mark, *Round-Trip to America, The Immigrants Return to Europe, 1880–1930*, New York, 1993

Zinn, Howard, *A People's History of the United States*, New York, 1999

Periodicals

Colliers Magazine
Holbrook Tribune-News
New York Times
Philadelphia Inquirer
The Times-Picayune

Websites

http://archive.scotsman.com
www.ancestry.com
www.dmm.org.uk
www.ggarchives.com/Maritime
www.gro.gov.uk
www.ncm.org.uk
www.newspaperarchive.com
www.nytimes.com/ref/membercenter/nytarchive.html
www.smithsonianmag.com

Acknowledgements

When I was a boy – about the same age as my grandfather when he returned from America – I was fixated on a book called *The Ship That Flew*. It was the story of a young boy who discovered a toy boat with magical qualities. It could transport him and his friends back to any point in time they wished to go. They naturally took full advantage of this facility and spent their weekends sailing off to Ancient Egypt, Norman Britain and Viking Scandinavia. Or at least, to the author's version of Ancient Egypt, Norman Britain and Viking Scandinavia . . .

It is now clear that large installments of my own adult life have been devoted to attempts to get back on the ship that flew, and this book is the latest example. So these acknowledgements wouldn't be valid if they didn't begin with acknowledging the abiding influence of Hilda Lewis, author of *The Ship That Flew*.

If Hilda, who died in 1974, was the skeleton at the bow, plenty of living people piloted me back to late 19th-century Durham and America. In England I am particularly grateful to Andy Bottomley, Arthur and Edith Dunn, Nan Hutchinson, Barbara Johnson, Jane Nelmes, Gwyneth and Derek Stubbs and Val Vayro. In the United States of America I would like to thank my guides Paul Barger, Rita Carter, Kathy Rich, Chris Rowley and David Smith. Thanks again to my agent, Stan, at Jenny Brown Associates. To Helen Bleck for some wonderfully sympathetic editing (I hardly felt the knife). And to Hugh Andrew, Jim Hutcheson, Sarah Morrison, Jan Rutherford and Andrew Simmons for the usual expert favours from Birlinn.

All the errors in what you have just read, and all of the dreams, are of course mine, not theirs. It's my ship.

Roger Hutchinson
July 2009